Davenport's Missouri Wills And Estate Planning Legal Forms

DAVENPORT'S MISSOURI WILLS AND ESTATE PLANNING LEGAL FORMS

2024 EDITION

written by attorneys
Alex Russell and Robert Maxwell

SEE BOOKS AND LEGAL FORMS AT
WWW.DAVENPORTPUBLISHING.COM

COPYRIGHT © 2024 -- ALEX RUSSELL

CREATIVE COMMONS LICENSE. This work is also licensed under a Creative Commons Attribution-NonCommercial-NoDerivatives 4.0 International License.

GOVERNMENT WORKS. No claim is made to copyright or ownership of government materials.

SOME STANDARD FORMS. No copyright or ownership is claimed of "standard" forms or leading forms for the state which are provided in this book, but fair use and privilege to use is claimed. Makers of such forms (often a state agency or hospital) have agreed by word, act, and implication the forms may be used and copied if no profit is sought and no substantial changes made to them. Such makers if not a lawyer or law firm are barred from profit or advantage in practicing law by making forms then limiting use. Forms and other related materials are used here for educational purposes only. Authors strongly believe in a religious duty to help people and do charity.

PUBLICATION DATA

(informal, library may use different data)

Names: Russell, Alex, 1972- author; Maxwell, Robert, 1960- author

Title: Davenport's Missouri Wills And Estate Planning Legal Forms 2024 Edition

Other Titles: Davenport's Wills

Description: Davenport Publishing 2024

Suggested Identifiers: 9798373194020
LCCN 2021909030
9798748423373

Subjects: LCSH: Wills--United States;
Wills--United States--Forms;
Estate Planning--United States;
Legal Forms

Classification: LFF KF755 .C55 2024 (or as library chooses)
DDC 346.73 Rus--dc24 (or as library chooses)

9 8 7 6 5 4 3 2 1 0 0 0 0 0 2 4

PERMISSION TO COPY AND USE BOOKS FOR FREE

To help people and groups publisher and authors of the book allow mostly free use by giving all a "Creative Commons Attribution-NonCommercial-NoDerivatives 4.0 International License".

Basically, as the image below says, any copying or use is OK if it still shows it is <u>by</u> the authors, is <u>non-commercial</u> (nc) with no price charged, and has <u>no derivatives (nd)</u> so no big changes.

Most users face no limit on copying, using, holding in library to loan out, or giving out copies.

Permission is given to change margins and formatting, do small changes, and cut any blank pages that may occur (but double-check page numbers and table of contents page numbers).

Printing on only 1 side of pages avoids complication of writing on back. Text margins are .75 inches. To do a book not a pamphlet increase left (inside) and decrease right (outside) margins.

Users can design a cover they like but the book title and author names must still appear on it.

Email questions to **davenportpress@gmail.com** .

(This work licensed under a Creative Commons Attribution-NonCommercial-NoDerivatives 4.0 International License.)

FOR FREE COPIES USE WWW.DAVENPORTPUBLISHING.COM OR BUY AT AMAZON.COM.

WARNING

THIS PUBLICATION IS NOT A SUBSTITUTE FOR LEGAL ADVICE. Publisher and authors say and warn this publication is not giving any legal, accounting, or other professional services or advice, which if wanted can be obtained by consulting in person an attorney or some other professional. **No attorney-client relationship or any relationship creating a duty or obligation is agreed to or created by the purchase or use of this publication or forms.**

BOOKS AND FORMS FOR OTHER STATES ARE AVAILABLE. SEE WWW.DAVENPORTPUBLISHING.COM FOR INFORMATION.

CHAPTER	TABLE OF CONTENTS	PAGE NUMBER
CHAPTER 1 – LIST OF FORMS, BOOK BASICS, AND INFORMATION FORM		1
CHAPTER 2 – LEGAL TERMS AND BASIC PROPERTY LAW		6
CHAPTER 3 – WILL BASICS		8
CHAPTER 4 – WILL GIFTS INCLUDING RESIDUE CLAUSE		10
CHAPTER 5 – DEBT, HOMESTEAD, MARRIAGE, AND CHILD ISSUES		15
CHAPTER 6 – BASIC IDEAS ABOUT HEALTH CARE FORMS		18

WILL RELATED FORMS

CHAPTER 7 – FORM 1: WILL (STANDARD)		19
CHAPTER 8 – FORM 2: WILL (GUARDIAN)		23
CHAPTER 9 – FORM 3: SELF-PROVING AFFIDAVIT		27
CHAPTER 10 – FORM 4: TANGIBLE PERSONAL PROPERTY MEMORANDUM		29

HEALTH CARE FORMS

CHAPTER 11 – FORM 5: DURABLE POWER OF ATTORNEY FOR HEALTH CARE AND/OR HEALTH CARE DIRECTIVE		31
CHAPTER 12 – FORM 6: DO NOT RESUSCITATE		36

GIVING POWER FORMS

CHAPTER 13 – FORM 7: DURABLE GENERAL POWER OF ATTORNEY		42
CHAPTER 14 – FORM 8: POWER OF ATTORNEY OVER MINOR CHILD		44
CHAPTER 15 – FORM 9: POWER OF ATTORNEY FOR RIGHT OF SEPULCHER OVER BODILY REMAINS		47
APPENDIX – SAMPLE FILLED OUT LEGAL FORMS		49

CHAPTER 1
LIST OF FORMS, BOOK BASICS, AND INFORMATION FORM

ESTATE PLANNING CONTROLS THINGS IF LATER ABSENT, SICK, OR DEAD
From Davenport Publishing this book covers "Estate Planning", which is a person doing legal documents now to control health care, property, money, children, and funeral if the person is later absent, sick, or dead.

ESTATE PLANNING MOSTLY IS DOING SIMPLE THINGS IN 3 AREAS
Estate Planning is mostly doing simple things in 3 areas: Will Related, Health Care, and Giving Power. This book has many legal forms specially made for Missouri. Most people use just a few of the forms.

WILL RELATED FORMS

Form 1. Will (Standard) – a Will (also called a "Last Will And Testament") lets a person control things after their death like who gets money and property, who is Executor, and if easier legal options can be used.

Form 2. Will (Guardian) – this is a Will with a part added to name a person to be Guardian to care for a minor child under 18 if needed (like if both parents later die) and also manage a child's property and money.

Form 3. Self-Proving Affidavit – optional form done with a Will to later help use a Will after a death.

Form 4. Tangible Personal Property Memorandum – lets a person easily add more gifts to a Will of gifts to happen after death, but this only covers "tangible personal property" like furniture, cars, and jewelry.

HEALTH CARE FORMS

Form 5. Durable Power Of Attorney For Health Care And/Or Health Care Directive – lets a person 1) name someone to control health care if needed (like if the person is later incapacitated by inability to stay conscious, communicate, or be rational), and 2) say whether to stop most care if later the doctors think more health care won't help an incapacitated person (called "Living Will" issues).

Form 6. Do Not Resuscitate – these are 2 forms that do serious act of immediately refusing most further care, and these are short so paramedics can read them fast and they can be used outside a care facility.

GIVING POWER FORMS

Form 7. Durable General Power Of Attorney – lets power over money, property, and other things be shared during a person's life with a trusted person like a spouse, adult child, or friend so they can do things.

Form 8. Power Of Attorney Over Minor Child – lets a parent share power over a child under 18 with someone so they have power to make decisions about health care and other things if ever needed.

Form 9. Power Of Attorney For Right Of Sepulcher Over Bodily Remains – lets a person give instructions and name a person to later after their death control their funeral and related matters.

MISSOURI LAW ON ESTATE PLANNING COVERS MOST PEOPLE HERE

This book is only for Missouri since Estate Planning laws and legal documents do vary between states. Usually a state's Estate Planning law applies if a person's primary residence is here (called their "domicile"). Many judges say "residence" occurs if a person lives in a place and has no clear plans to leave. Later plans to move don't matter till people move. People can stay under a previous state's Estate Planning laws after they move if people always plan to leave any new state. So people who temporarily move to a new state for school, work, or military might say they are keeping legal ties to their old state. Note, people often do health care forms for the state a health facility is in. Most immigrants of any kind can do Estate Planning here.

PERSON HAS POWER TO CONTROL THESE THINGS BUT IT'S OFTEN NOT VITAL

Estate Planning to control health care, property, money, children, funeral, and similar things if a person is absent, sick, or dead is usually easy to do because a person legally has full power to control these things. Given this usually judges, doctors, and other people mostly just ask: "Based on what a person wrote what did they likely want done?" It is also easy to do because simple legal documents can do the things and simple words can also be used (like listing some property and putting a few names). Despite what many people say often Estate Planning is not worth a lot of effort or money since it often does not greatly change costs, taxes, delays, and later work needed in these areas. Benefits seem especially low for young people since only 4% of people die by age 50, and only 0.2% of children before age 18 have 2 parents die to need big legal help. *See Social Security Standard Tables by Felicitie Bell; Parent Mortality Census SIPP Study Paper #288.* Many people spend more energy and money on getting good life insurance to help family and friends.

BOOK IS SHORT, HAS FORMS TO QUICKLY SEE, AND USES EMPHASIS

This book is short and may read rough but can be read fast, and long books can cause misunderstanding of the basics and skimming. This book quickly tries to show many legal forms. For emphasis paragraph titles, boxes, and underlining is used. To save space some small words are skipped and end quote marks are put before punctuation. This book capitalizes some legal words like Will, Testator, and Agent but this is optional.

THIS BOOK COVERS MAIN LEGAL IDEAS AND SHOULD SUIT MOST PEOPLE

This book covers the main U.S. legal ideas on Estate Planning and major ways Missouri law is different. This book can't cover all legal issues but should suit most people without some strange situations or wishes. Strange situations or wishes that may need research or a lawyer include: a) strange gift wishes for property and money, b) wealth over $5 million, c) big medical concerns like extreme age, d) property or money going to a person with a disability or special needs, and e) wish to move or hide assets to qualify for government help.

LEGAL FORMS CAN HELP MANY AND THIS BOOK HAS STANDARD FORMS

Legal forms are good at most things involved in Estate Planning and can make binding legal documents. Instead of legal forms a lawyer can be used for Estate Planning but this can be costly, take months of work, and they can make mistakes. In life people often pick a cheaper option. Importantly, often a hospital, charity, state agency, or state legislature has made a form most people use and call the "standard form", and doctors, judges, and other people may not like to follow anything else. This book does provide mostly standard forms.

DOCUMENTS MAY NEED TO BE WITNESSED, NOTARIZED, AND USED RIGHT

To be legally enforceable certain legal documents need to be "witnessed", which is someone watching the person doing the form sign and then the witness signs too. Some documents to be enforceable need to be "notarized" which means a person who is a "notary" sees it signed and then uses an ink stamp and signs. Persons who are a notary (also called a "notary public") are at some banks, brokers, insurance agents, courts, law offices, libraries, and mail-copy centers. Some notaries can be found by calling using a local phonebook. The words "subscribe" and "execute" means a person signed a document, and "acknowledgment" means a person said a signature was theirs. If a person signs a document in a foreign language it is usually binding. When filling in a form it may help people to know "respectively" in a form means "in the order just stated". When filling out a legal form except for signatures the other parts can be filled in by a person not doing the form and using pencil is even allowed for this. Once done often people try to keep the original document and hand out copies. Some people have everyone sign multiple copies to have many copies with ink signatures.

SOME LESS COMMON OR LESS USEFUL FORMS ARE NOT IN THIS BOOK

This book skips some possible but less common or less useful documents.

- ■ A "Codicil" can modify or add to a Will but it is easier and legally safer to just rewrite the whole Will.
- ■ Some people do a "Pet Trust" to help a pet, but it's easier to just give money in Will to person given a pet.
- ■ Some people do a "Revocable Living Trust" so a Trust entity with a Trustee holds property or money during their life, usually done to after death have faster transfer of things and to avoid small delays, costs, or work for others (by "avoiding probate"). But this is rare as it may require moving most of a person's things to a Trust causing maybe years of hassle, mostly to avoid later small work for people happy to be getting things.
- ■ "Childrens Trust" papers can be done so upon a death a Trust gets things for a minor child to manage till 18, but this is rarely done due to possible costs and hassles and since it rarely matters (as this book explains).
- ■ Though separate forms exist usually organ donation in handled in drivers license or state ID paperwork.

USUALLY NO FEDERAL, MISSOURI, OR OTHER TAX IS OWED AT A DEATH

Despite what many people think usually no tax is owed due to a death, including no inheritance, estate, or similar taxes. The "Federal Estate And Gift Tax" is only owed if a tax credit is used up that covers $13.61 million a person after 2023. Missouri and its counties and cities no longer impose any tax upon a death, including any estate, inheritance, or similar taxes. A few states have taxes that may apply for property there if the owner dies, but they usually do not tax anything if the total is under $3 million.

PROBABLY DO NEW DOCUMENTS IF DIVORCE, MARRY, HAVE CHILD, OR MOVE

Divorcing, marrying, having a new child, or moving to a new state can have big legal effects, and if any of these events occur it is recommended people do a new Will and other Estate Planning papers soon. To help most states say a Will from another state is still valid if people move but this is not always certain.

INFORMATION FORM CAN HELP TELL FAMILY AND FRIENDS THINGS

Many people do some kind of "Information Form" so family or friends after a death know helpful things. People can staple financial records and other pages to this. See form on the next pages to use if wanted.

ESTATE PLANNING HELPFUL INFORMATION

For more space attach copies of form or blank pages. Keep pages by Will or other place for Executor or family.

1. Personal Information (Name, Birthdate, Social Security number, special family details, other):

2. Real estate, vehicles, and other major tangible property (especially if people may not find them):

3. Non-tangible assets like stocks, accounts, investments, loans owed you, and business interests:

4. Possible income or insurance like pensions, retirement, disability, insurance, or contracts:

5. Debts owed by you like credit card, loan, student loan, mortgage, car loans, and accounts payable:

6. Names and information of professionals used (attorneys, accountants, brokers, doctors, others):

7. Computer passwords and helpful files, document places, and safes or safe-deposit boxes code/key:

8. Other helpful things, wishes for funeral, special requests, and last messages to family and friends:

CHAPTER 2
LEGAL TERMS AND BASIC PROPERTY LAW

THERE ARE BASIC LEGAL TERMS AND IDEAS IN ESTATE PLANNING

Some legal terms and ideas are basic to Estate Planning.

■ "Estate Planning" is about people doing legal documents to control things if later absent, sick, or dead. After a document is done people are mostly free to sell or transfer property, instruct doctors, or change forms.

■ A "person doing a legal document" and "doing a form" means the form is for and affects that person.

■ "Probate" is a legal process to do things after someone's death like transfer property, handle creditors, and authorize a Guardian. Due to changes in the law probate is now often informal, faster, and less costly.

■ A "Will" or "will" (this book uses upper case "W") is a legal document done to control issues after death. The phrase "Last Will And Testament" is used since a "Testament" long ago was a small document done along with a Will to do some things. After a death Wills are filed in the Probate Division at Circuit Court.

■ A person doing a Will is called "Testator" or "Will maker". Before about 1995 a woman Testator was called a "Testatrix" and woman Executor called an "Executrix" but this is no longer often said or written.

■ If no valid Will is done a person is "intestate" and then a dead person's property and money is transferred to a spouse, children, and family as intestate law says. Some people a fine with this. This is covered later.

■ A person who died is called the "decedent" or "deceased". A person getting a Will gift is called a "recipient", "beneficiary", or "heir" if related (they "inherit"). "Survive" or "surviving" is to be alive after someone else died. The term "descendants" or "issue" usually means a person's children and grandchildren.

■ A person named in a Will to handle things after someone's death is called an "Executor", but if a judge has to pick someone they are called an "Administrator". The new term "Personal Representative" covers both these things and this new term is now commonly used in most Wills in Missouri.

■ Legally property is: 1) "real property" which is land and buildings ("real estate"), 2) "fixtures" which are things tied to real property (like fences, carpets, and wired-in appliances), or 3) "personal property" which is everything else (like household items, clothes, tools, cars, jewelry, art, moneys, accounts, and stocks),

■ A person under 18 is usually called a "minor" and often a parent or guardian helps them do things. A minor or other person not reasonably able to make wise decisions lacks "capacity" and is "incapacitated".

■ A document giving power to someone is often called a "Power of Attorney" where the "Principal" gives power to someone called the "Agent" or "Attorney-in-Fact" (but they needn't be a real attorney or a lawyer).

■ Missouri law is the Missouri Revised Statutes ("revised" means updated). Each law is called a "statute" or "section" usually shown by a "§" symbol. An example of how to refer to a law is: "Mo. Rev. Stat. § 104.33". A legal form written by the legislature into state law for people to use if wanted is called a "statutory form".

ESTATE MEANS PROPERTY OF DECEDENT AND ENTITY HOLDING THINGS

The "estate" or "probate estate" means all property and money of a dead person that at death or soon after didn't automatically legally go to new owners. Estate is also the name for a temporary entity run by an Executor to do things after a death (it's like a small corporation, e.g., "Estate of John Alan Smith").

PERSON CAN ONLY GIFT IN WILL WHAT THEY OWN AT DEATH

A person can only gift by Will things they own at death, so people should research what they do own. Basically by law a person usually owns all they earn as wages and salary, owns their share of income and profit tied to property they own, and owns or partly owns any things their money buys or improves. And for property with "title" documents (real estate or vehicles) or where there is a "listed owner" (like accounts) the named persons are usually the legal owners unless evidence shows special circumstances. Note, a person during life can sell property, make gifts, or transfer things even if they are named in a Will, so people should consider if they already sold or gave away property they also name in a Will gift.

NON-PROBATE TRANSFERS THAT HAPPEN AUTOMATICALLY IGNORE A WILL

It is vital to be aware some money or property of a decedent may automatically transfer on death or soon after to new owners if certain arrangements were made earlier. This is usually called "non-probate property". Such things transfer as arranged even if a Will names the same items in some Will gifts.

Examples are: a) a "designated beneficiary" form was done to name people to get an investment or account, b) transfer-on-death accounts were used, and c) real property is held by 2 people as "joint tenants with survivorship" or similar so at a death the surviving person gets things. Also, usually property in a Trust will ignore a Will and transfer as Trust papers say to. Life insurance usually goes to the named beneficiary.

Trying to do non-probate transfers for all things is called "avoiding probate", but few people try this since it can cause years of hassle, benefits are small, and often some thing is missed. When doing a Will people should consider non-probate transfers that will occur automatically at a death and consider what will be left.

THINGS OWNED IN SPECIAL WAYS MAY LIMIT GIFTING IN WILL

A person should consider if they own real estate or other property in special ownership ways which may limit gifting by Will. Laws vary in different states but some common special ways of ownership are:

- "joint tenant with right of survivorship" or similar legal options may be used in papers, so at a death property goes automatically to other named owners despite what a Will says (this is often how spouses hold a home);
- papers say a "life estate" exists, so then if someone dies the other people in papers the get an item; and
- "Trust property" occurs if paperwork made a Trust entity and then property was transferred into it or this is set to occur, so then the Trust papers control where things put in the Trust go after someone's death.

Simple "joint ownership" with many owners can occur if people do joint papers, all agree to it, buy with joint funds, or if a gift was to many people. Wills can gift joint property, like "I give my half of boat to Ed Hu".

CHAPTER 3
WILL BASICS

A WILL LETS A PERSON CONTROL THINGS AFTER THEIR DEATH

A Will is a legal document done by a person to control some things after their death. A person doing a Will is called the "Testator" or "Will maker". In Missouri a Testator when signing a Will must be at least age 18, of sound mind (rational with sufficient memory), and not be under duress (unfair pressure or threat).

KEEP SIGNED WILL IN SAFE PLACE IT CAN BE FOUND AFTER A DEATH

A Will should be kept so it can be found within days of a death, like in a desk, drawer, safe, with a person, or rarely a safe deposit box. Family can be told how to find a Will. Though rarely done a living person can file a Will at court for safekeeping, and later family or an Executor can withdraw it. Mo. Rev. Stat. § 474.510.

A WILL MUST BE SIGNED WITH 2 WITNESSES

A WILL TO BE VALID USUALLY MUST BE SIGNED WITH 2 WITNESSES

In Missouri a document to be a Will must show it is a Will and the person doing it usually must sign in front of at least 2 persons acting as witnesses who then sign too. A Will just spoken on a video or audio recording usually has no legal effect. Unlike some states Missouri does not let Will witnesses be skipped just because a Will is handwritten. Some people modify a Will to have 3 or 4 witnesses in case this helps later.

WITNESSES SHOULD BE AT LEAST AGE 18 AND NOT GETTING WILL GIFTS

A person to witness a Will must be at least 18. Under Missouri law a Will is valid if witnesses are getting gifts in the Will or benefitting other ways, but normally these gifts are void and won't later be carried out unless there are 2 other proper witnesses. A small exception says close family can still get by Will up to the amount they'd have got under state law if there were no Will. Mo. Rev. Stat. § 474.330. Most people try to pick witnesses who are "disinterested" which means they or any spouse are not getting things in a Will. It is best but not legally required a witness not be very old, live far away, or be named in a Will to be Executor, Guardian, or similar position. Usually witnesses for a Will are friends, strangers, or distant family.

TESTATOR AND 2 WITNESSES SIGN THE WILL WHEN TOGETHER IN 1 ROOM

A person doing a Will usually signs it with at 2 witnesses who also sign while all are in 1 room and seeing others sign. A Testator and witnesses should use their full legal name unless they dislike and rarely use it. People showing others an ID is common but not required. Often witnesses print their name and address. Witnesses only read the 1 paragraph of the Will they sign. A Testator need not initial all of the Will pages. By law witnesses must know a document is a Will and someone should tell them this. Though not required often a Testator says a thing like: "My name is _____ and this is my Will I do voluntarily and ask you 2 people to witness". Some Testators chat a bit with witnesses about a Will to show they are of sound mind.

MOST WILLS SAY PEOPLE MAY LATER DO INFORMAL PROBATE

Most Wills say after a death the family and friends may do "informal probate" which can avoid costs and delays. Informal probate often is done with just 1 court hearing and often is completed in well under 1 year.

MOST WILLS SAY TO SKIP COSTLY BOND FOR EXECUTOR AND OTHERS

Most Wills helpfully say no "bond" or "surety" is required for any Executor, Guardian, or similar persons. A bond is insurance from a company to insure against misconduct. A Testator usually doesn't want a bond since the persons Testator names are trusted and them later needing a bond will cost the estate money.

CANCELING OLD WILLS IS USUALLY NOT A PROBLEM

So a new Will is followed old Wills should be canceled ("revoked"). To do this a new Will in the first part usually says old Wills are revoked. Or people can revoke a Will by marking it, like with "void" or a giant "X". Usually crossing out just part of a Will has no effect. Revoking a Will usually doesn't bring back an earlier Will.

OFTEN AT START OF A WILL A PERSON NAMES ANY SPOUSE AND CHILDREN

Many Wills start with a place for a Testator to name any current living spouse and children of any age. Natural or adopted children should be put here including any born outside of marriage. People without this family can skip this or just write "none". Not doing this may invalidate a Will by indicating a person lacks sufficient mental ability, or let a spouse or child not listed ask a judge to give them a share or all of the estate by claiming a Testator forgot them. After listing family in a Will a Testator is often free to give them nothing.

A WILL NAMES AN EXECUTOR TO DO THINGS AFTER DEATH

A WILL NAMES SOMEONE TO BE EXECUTOR TO DO THINGS AFTER A DEATH

Usually a Will names someone as "Executor" to act after a death. The law gives Executors many helpful legal powers, like to handle debts, find and collect and give new owners property and money, and do probate If a Will fails to name an Executor a judge can pick someone, but family may argue about who to suggest. Note, the term "Personal Representative" and not Executor is now often used in Missouri for the person doing things after a death, but these terms mostly mean the same thing. Will gifts can go to an Executor.

EXECUTOR CAN BE PAID AND ESTATE PAYS FOR EXECUTOR'S EXPENSES

Missouri law says an Executor can ask to can be paid for their work, and the law basically lets them ask to be paid about 3% of estate property and money. Mo. Rev. Stat. § 473.153. But usually most Executors later skip asking for pay so as to not owe income tax and leave more resources to carry out more Will gifts. Costs any Executor has like for insurance, utilities, repairs, funeral, mortgage, attorneys, and probate costs are paid for with money or property of the estate. Any lawyer hired is paid what they and Executor agree on which may be an hourly rate or, also, sometimes the same percentage of the estate the Executor may get.

EXECUTOR MUST BE AT LEAST 18 AND SECOND PERSON RARELY IS NEEDED

A person to be Executor must be at least age 18 and usually a judge later can't find they have a bad criminal record like a felony. A non-resident can be Executor but they must name someone local to get mail. Naming 2 people to both be Executor is allowed but rare due to the risk of arguments and delays, and since any 1 person named should be trusted. People can name a 2nd fallback person to be Executor just in case the 1st person isn't available but most skip this since this is rare and if needed a judge can pick someone. To add such a 2nd person a person could add: "or if they're reasonably unable to serve I name ___ to serve".

CHAPTER 4
WILL GIFTS INCLUDING RESIDUE CLAUSE

MAIN USE OF A WILL IS TO WRITE GIFTS TO HAPPEN AFTER DEATH
Most people use a Will mainly to legally say what happens to their property and money after their death, usually by writing down various Will gifts to occur when they die. Verbal and even writings about this are not usually valid if not in a written Will. A Will can control property acquired after it was signed. The end of this chapter covers "intestate law" which says where a person's things go at death if no valid Will handles this.

GIFTING IN A WILL USING SIMPLE WORDS OFTEN IS BEST
Making gifts in a Will using simple words is often best, using words like "I give to" and "I gift to". This is legally fine and avoids confusing legal words like "bequest", "devise", and "legacy" which few people know.

A PERSON IS MOSTLY FREE TO GIFT THEIR THINGS AS WANTED
A person is mostly free to give at death their money and property as they want. But creditors a decedent owed money, a spouse, and minor children under age 18 may have some rights which this book later covers.

IN WILL CAN DO SPECIFIC GIFTS TO GIFT PARTICULAR PROPERTY
Most Wills have "specific gifts" to gift <u>particular things</u>. Specific gifts can be any property, like "I give boat to Ed Blom" and "I give UBank account #84553873 to Sue Wu". If a gift is not clear the law assumes all of a kind of thing is given, like "I give jewelry to Ann Po" means <u>all</u> jewelry. But gifting specific property can have surprises like value of items can change, or a Will gift may later fail to occur if property is not owned at death.

IN WILL CAN DO GENERAL GIFTS LIKE OF MONEY
Wills can do "general gifts" where what is gifted is not particular property but can be flexibly chosen, like "I give 1 of my 3 cars to Ed Po" which lets an Executor pick which car. The usual general gift is money, like "I give $5 to Ed Hu". Money gifts are easy to write, let equal gifts be made, and are legally safer for many reasons. To carry out money gifts an Executor usually uses accounts or sells some property in the estate.

PERSON IN WILL GIFT USUALLY MUST SURVIVE OR GIFT DOES NOT OCCUR
Many Wills like this book's Will forms say a person named in a Will gift must survive (live past) the Testator for the gift to occur unless gift language specifically says different. If survival is not required for a Will gift then what happens if a person named in a Will gift later dies before Testator can be legally unclear. <u>People doing a Will should consider how Will gifts to people dying before Testator usually have no effect</u>. People if they see a person in a Will gift has died can re-do a Will or just let the Residue Clause handle it.

RESIDUE CLAUSE IS CATCH-ALL THAT HELPFULLY GIFTS ANYTHING LEFT
This chapter later covers how a Residue Clause in Will gifts property or money not already gifted or used.

LATER DIVORCE OR MURDER CANCELS WILL GIFTS TO THE ACTING PERSON
If a person divorces or murders a Testator then by state law usually all Will gifts to them are cancelled.

GIFTS IN WILL CAN GO TO A GROUP OR CLASS OF PEOPLE

To save work a Will gift can go to a group or class of people like certain family <u>if who is meant is later easy to determine</u>. People can say roughly how <u>much in total</u> is gifted to be clearer. Examples are: "I give $10 to each person on my 2018 soccer team" and "I give $10 to each of my grandkids so this is about $100 in total."

CAN SAY IF PERSON IN GIFT DIES THEN IT GOES TO LINEAL DESCENDANTS

A Will gift can say it goes to a person but if they don't survive then to their "lineal descendants per stirpes". Descendants are a person's children and grandchildren. "Per stirpes" means "by branch" and is about how to spread property and money, and it mostly tries to divide things so <u>each family branch gets an equal share</u>. Most Wills use "lineal descendants" language in a Residue Clause. <u>An example shows how it works</u>:

A Will may say: **"Clothes to Sue Wu but if they don't survive to their lineal descendants per stirpes"**, and this means if Sue Wu has died and her son Ken Wu is living and her other son Ben Wu has died but left 2 children then, legally, by law Ken Wu himself gets 50% and Ben Wu's 2 children each get 25%.

GIFT RECIPIENTS DYING BEFORE TESTATOR IS RARE AND EASY TO HANDLE

Having a person named in a Will gift die is rare and usually noticed and then <u>people often re-do a Will to replace any dead person in Will gifts</u>, or some people don't act and trust a Residue Clause to handle it.

PEOPLE CAN ADD AN ALTERNATE BENEFICIARY LIKE FOR SPECIAL ITEMS

Some people for the small risk a recipient in a Will gift dies before a Testaror, and maybe for special items, <u>write a bit to add an "alternate beneficiary"</u>, like "I give boat to Ed Fox but if they don't survive me to Ann Fox".

GIFT BENEFICIARIES CAN GET PERCENTAGE RATHER THAN EQUAL SHARE

If a Will gift goes to multiple people the law assumes equal shares, but if wanted percentages can be used to make unequal gifts, like "I give boat 90% to John Smith and 10% to Mary Baker".

PROPERTY OR MONEY IN A JOINT GIFT GOES TO MULTIPLE PEOPLE

The same property or money can go to many people to each get a part, and this is called a "joint gift". For example, "I give boat and all hats to Ann Baxter and Mary Ann Swanson" means each person owns part of every item. People later can split things by agreement or an Executor can decide how to divide items. If a person in a joint gift has died their part usually is left to transfer under a Residue Clause.

AFTER A DEATH FAMILIES OFTEN LET PEOPLE TAKE ITEMS UNOFFICIALLY

Many families let people take items <u>unofficially</u> in ways a person said, wrote on notes, or showed by stickers. This often works out fine. If anyone officially objects a judge will have a Will and law be followed, but later people can voluntarily retransfer items. <u>This book later covers how to gift by Tangible Personal Property Memorandum</u>.

CAN LEAVE SOME WILL GIFT AREAS BLANK OR WRITE TO SAY SKIP GIFTS

A person can choose to not use some gifts areas in a Will legal form, like by just leaving areas blank, writing things like "SKIPPED" or "NONE", or using a computer to delete some gift lines. Judges and others usually do not care about neatness or empty spaces in Wills, and will follow whatever parts are filled in.

RESIDUE CLAUSE GIFTING ANYTHING LEFT IS MAIN WAY TO GIFT THINGS

THE RESIDUE CLAUSE IS A CATCH-ALL THAT GIFTS ANYTHING LEFT

Most Wills by the end have a Residue Clause to give property or money left in a person's estate not gifted earlier in a Will or used other ways. All that is left this way is called the "Residue". Many people let this clause handle most things. This avoids all need to list and describe property and money and also has less legal risk.

USUAL RESIDUE CLAUSE HAS 2 PARTS

A short 2 part Residue Clause is usual and is used in this book's Will forms, and it has:

1) a 1st space to name persons to get things if they survive the Testator (many name a spouse or closest family here), and if several people are named here but only some survive the survivors split things, and

2) a 2nd space to name persons to get things if all in the 1st space don't survive (many people name next closest family or friends here), and if a person in the 2nd space has died their descendants get their share.

EXAMPLE OF 2 PART RESIDUE CLAUSE:

"RESIDUE CLAUSE: The rest, residue, and remainder of my estate, and anything else, I give to:

  a) to   __John Doe my husband__   who survive me and with persons just named who survive me taking the share of non-survivors, then if anything remains

  b) to   __Sam Doe, Ann Wu, and Pam Ax__   and if any of those just named do not survive me their part goes to their lineal descendants per stirpes."

In this example if John Doe has survived he gets everything. If John Doe hasn't survived and also Sam Doe hasn't survived but he left 2 children then, legally, Sam's 2 children split the 1/3 share of his (so get 1/6 each) and the other 2 persons in 2nd part (Ann Wu and Pam Ax) get 1/3 each. Usually the first people named in the clause won't die so gets things, and if they are seen to have died a Will can be redone.

SOME PEOPLE USE PERCENTAGES TO GIFT DIFFERENT AMOUNTS OF RESIDUE

Some people use percentages in a Residue Clause to get the exact split wanted. This can gift a lot (like to a person's children) and gift a small bit (like to a grandchild or more distant people). *See example in Appendix.*

SOME PEOPLE WRITE THE SAME THING IN BOTH PARTS OR SKIP A PART

Some people put the same names in both clause spaces or skip part of it to do some things. For example, a person with no spouse may skip the 1st part and in 2nd part name their children (including any who died who had kids of their own) so all branches of a person's descendants get a share. *See example in Appendix.*

SOME PEOPLE CHANGE A RESIDUE CLAUSE TO HAVE 1 PART

Some people change a Residue Clause to have just 1 part since this can gift more equally and be easier to understand. *See example in Appendix.* For example a Residue Clause can be made to say:

"The rest, residue, and remainder of my estate, and anything else, I give to: _____ who survive me and if any of those just named do not survive me their part goes to their lineal descendants per stirpes."

MUST SUFFICIENTLY DESCRIBE NAMES AND PROPERTY IN A WILL

PUTTING NAMES OF PEOPLE OR GROUPS IN A WILL IS FAIRLY EASY

Putting names in a Will is fairly easy. Later a judge or Executor assume a person putting names in a Will meant to gift to people they know, so common names are OK unless 2 friends or family use the same name. Details can help if names won't be recognized or to be friendly, like "I give $5 to my nurse Sue Smith" and "I give $5 to loyal pal Ed Dutton". If people mostly used a nickname "also known as" or "a/k/a" may help, like "I give $5 to Dan Smith a/k/a Big Red". Gifts can go to a charity, a government, or a group, like "I give $8 to Goodwill Charities, "I give $8 to the Library of Cole County, MO", and "I give $8 to Plum Church, Dallas, TX". People sometimes phone to learn a charity's or organization's correct name.

PUTTING DESCRIPTIONS OF ITEMS IN WILL GIFTS IS FAIRLY EASY

Describing items in gifts is fairly easy. Later a judge or Executor assume a person in a Will meant to gift items they own, and rarely do people own similar things so there is later confusion. Often OK is doing gifts with simple words like: "I give ax to Ed Wu" and "I give big table to Jed Fox". It's OK to gift by category or a list, like: "I give tools to Sam Lee" and "I give cow, van, and harp to Sue Po". For financial items plain words can be used, like "I give bank accounts and stocks to Ann Bima", or details can be used, like: "I give Wells Fargo bank account ending 8714 to Tom Hud". Gifting using a location is riskier as judges will ignore a Will gift if it seems items were placed to affect gifting and for no "independently significant" life reason. So, "I give Ed Po items in my desk and safe" a judge might not follow but "I give Ed Po hats at cabin" likely is OK.

DESCRIBING REAL PROPERTY IS HARD IF NOT USING RESIDUE OR TITLE

Gifting real property (real estate) at death can be hard to do and the legally safer way to do this is:
1) do nothing specific so it's handled by a Will Residue Clause, or 2) have a lawyer or agent put names in a deed or other document for the real property so then named persons legally get things at someone's death.

Gifting real property at death other ways is harder. Helpfully a gift of real property using a location by law gifts all land, buildings, and fixtures located there with no need to list the buildings, fixtures, and land.

It is possible to gift real property at a particular address with very plain words, like a house, fixtures, and land can be fully given by something like: "I give 86 Maxwell Street, St. Louis, Missouri, to Mary Ann Brown".

People can do a blanket gift giving all of a kind of property, like, "I give all real property and fixtures in Clay County, Missouri to Ann Ivy Hill " or "I give all real property and fixtures to Eric Paul Carlson".

Giving real property in a Will using a "legal description" is how many lawyers do it, but this can be hard to do. If using a legal description people must write without mistakes the full legal description of maybe many lines into a Will with no abbreviation at all. A legal description might be found on a deed or on mortgage papers. Legal descriptions may refer to a "lot" or "blocks" on a map which is recorded in land records of a county, or it may refer to a path around the land borders with various angles, distances, and iron stakes.

CONDITIONS ON WILL GIFTS ARE RARE DUE TO POSSIBLE PROBLEMS
Putting conditions on a gift, like "I give Ann Poe $90 if she graduates college", can cause problems like years of delay, risk of lawsuits, and big attorney's fees. Due to all this conditions are rarely put on Will gifts.

MOST STATES AND WILLS SAY PEOPLE TO GET GIFTS MUST SURVIVE 5 DAYS
Helpful laws in most states and all this book's Will forms say if a person dies within 5 days (120 hours) of a Testator or simultaneously, then they are legally seen as dying before the Testator. This skips the need to prove exact time of death (like if people die in 1 accident), and avoids a Will gift or right to something going to someone who then soon dies within days (so an item may have to go through multiple probate proceedings).

MOST WILLS HAVE A MISCELLANEOUS PART WITH HELPFUL LANGUAGE
Most Wills have a "Miscellaneous" page with legal language that might help avoid later legal problems.

INTESTATE LAW COVERS PROPERTY OR MONEY NOT HANDLED BY WILL

INTESTATE LAW CONTROLS THINGS NOT HANDLED BY A WILL
Missouri "intestate law" which starts at Mo. Rev. Stat. § 474.010 says <u>if a person dies with no valid Will</u> or <u>if anything is left after Will and all transfers are done</u> then some surviving (living) family get property and money left by the person who died (their "estate"). Many people are fine with what intestate law says and choose to skip a Will, but often doing a Will has some other benefits like later avoiding some costs or delays. Note, "descendants" and "issue" both mean a person's children and grandchildren, and if a person dies who would've got an intestate share often their descendants get that share. State intestate law says as follows:

474.010. General rules of descent. — All property as to which any decedent dies intestate [the estate] shall descend and be distributed, subject to the payment of claims, as follows:

(1) The surviving spouse shall receive:
    (a) The entire intestate estate if there is no surviving issue [descendants] of the decedent;
    (b) The first $20,000 in value of the intestate estate, plus one-half of the balance of the intestate estate, if there are surviving issue, all of whom are also issue of the surviving spouse;
    (c) One-half of the intestate estate if there are surviving issue, one or more of whom are not issue of the surviving spouse;

(2) The part not distributable to the surviving spouse [...] shall descend and be distributed as follows:
    (a) To the decedent's children, or their descendants, in equal parts;
    (b) If there are no children, or their descendants, then to the decedent's father, mother, brothers and sisters or their descendants in equal parts;
    (c) If there are no children, or their descendants, father, mother, brother or sister, or their descendants, then to the grandfathers, grandmothers, uncles and aunts or their descendants;
    (d) If there are [none of the above surviving, then to more distant relatives to a reasonable degree];

(3) If there is no surviving spouse or kindred of the decedent entitled to inherit, the whole shall go to the kindred of the predeceased spouse [.]

(4) If no person is entitled to inherit as stated in this section the property shall [be forfeited to Missouri].

CHAPTER 5
DEBT, HOMESTEAD, MARRIAGE, AND CHILD ISSUES

THIS CHAPTER COVERS CERTAIN ISSUES THAT SOME PEOPLE CAN SKIP
This chapter covers debt, marriage, and young child issues, and some people can skip parts of this.

DEBT ISSUES

PAYING DECEDENT'S DEBTS MAY USE UP RESOURCES AND REDUCE GIFTS
If a decedent had debts then creditors owed may ask a judge to be paid from decedent's money or property before Will gifts and certain transfers occur. How debts are paid is set by state law and a Will need not describe this. Funds to pay debts comes from decedent's money and property so may affect (in order) the Will Residue, Will general gifts, Will specific gifts, and non-probate transfers. Probate, health care, taxes, and funeral costs by law have some priority to be paid first. For certain reasons often not all debts are paid. People should consider how paying debts may use up money or property, leaving less to carry out Will gifts. A spouse and family usually aren't liable for decedent's debts unless they actually guaranteed or co-signed.

SECURED DEBTS LIKE MORTGAGE OR VEHICLE LIEN ARE NOT PAID OFF
Laws in most states say do not pay off any secured debts on property of a decedent like a house mortgage or vehicle lien even if other debts are paid by Executor or in probate. This avoids using up estate resources on paying these usually big debts and leaves more estate resources to carry out Will gifts and other transfers. Due to this, all this book's Will forms say do not usually pay off any secured debts. But if a Testator wants they can 1) put in a Will an order to pay (like, "Executor pay off the house mortgage"), or 2) gift ample enough money to pay off a secured debt to the person getting the property. Most banks let the new owners after a death keep paying monthly any secured debt like a mortgage or lien.

FAMILY RIGHTS MAY BE USED TO GET FAMILY THINGS BEFORE DEBTS
Most states have "Family Rights" a decedent's surviving spouse or children can claim, and this helpfully may let them get things even before most debts of decedent are paid and even before Will gifts.

First, in many U.S. states a surviving spouse or children can use an "Exempt Property" right to get some of decedent's clothing and household items to let family comfortably live. In Missouri a spouse (or if there's no spouse the dependent children) can get a large part of decedent's clothing, appliances, furniture, and 1 vehicle. See Mo. Rev. Stat. § 474.250. Family also can try to get more by claiming in life decedent gave them things.

Second, in many U.S. states a surviving spouse or dependent children can use a "Family Allowance" right to get some of a decedent's money and property to live on for 1 year or so. In Missouri often $24,000 can be claimed for this, or a higher amount up to $80,000 upon a showing of need. See Mo. Rev. Stat. § 474.260.

Third, in many U.S. states if a decedent left a small estate the family can use a "Small Estate Affidavit" to get most of what there is. Missouri also does this, and in Missouri a decedent's family can usually use an affidavit to get all a decedent left if there is under $40,000 of money and property.

So family don't cause legal trouble by using these rights usually a person by Will or other way gives over 50% and any main family house to any spouse or small children. Some people may want to do more research.

HOMESTEAD ISSUES

In many states a surviving spouse or young children have some right to get (or just stay in for years) the house or mobile home owned by a decedent under a "Homestead Law". But Missouri law mostly does not say a spouse or children will get this. Missouri law just gives a spouse or dependent children a right to a further $15,000 of a decedent's things or money under the "Homestead Allowance". See Mo. Rev. Stat. § 474.290. But a person who owns a home and has a spouse or small children can do papers so the spouse or children will get ownership automatically of the home, including by making them "joint tenants" in the land records. Note, so family don't try to cause legal trouble about a house usually a person gives any home to any spouse or young children. Some people may want to do other research.

MARRIAGE ISSUES

MISSOURI USES SEPARATE PROPERTY LAW FOR SPOUSES

Missouri like most states uses the Separate Property Law system that says a married person mostly owns their money and property separately and not jointly with a spouse. Due to this a married person is usually free to sell during life or gift by Will most of their money or property and not have to involve a spouse. But joint ownership by 2 spouses and not separate ownership can arise in other ways, like by agreement, both spouses paying part of the purchase price, if a gift was to both spouses, or if paperwork calls it joint.

COMMUNITY PROPERTY LAW APPLIES IN OTHER STATES FOR SPOUSES

There are 9 states mostly in the Western U.S. that use the Community Property Law system for spouses (Arizona, California, Louisiana, Idaho, Nevada, New Mexico, Texas, Washington, and Wisconsin). This says property or money is owned 50/50 by spouses as Community Property if it's from mental or physical work while married (like wages or salary) or if items are bought or improved with any other Community Property. People recently moving from these states may face legal issues.

JOINT WILL OR SIMILAR BOTH SPOUSES SIGN IS NOT RECOMMENDED

Some couples who worry a lot try to sign a "Joint Will" or a "Contract To Make A Will" done by a lawyer which says spouses give all to the other if they die first, then says last living spouse gives to all children equally, and usually says a spouse may not change this. This is banned in some states and is rarely used.

SPOUSE CAN GET ELECTIVE 1/2 OR 1/3 SHARE INSTEAD OF FOLLOWING WILL

A spouse if unhappy with what a Will and other transfers may give them has a right to instead choose (elect) an "Elective Share" of a share of a dead spouse's property and money rather than them take what a Will says. States do this for fairness, so a spouse has resources to live on, and so early divorce isn't the only way to be financially secure. To avoid this both spouses would have to do a pre-nuptial or similar agreement by a lawyer which is rare. Missouri sets the Elective Share at 1/2 of money and property in decedent's estate, or 1/3 of this if decedent left any descendants like child or grandchild. See Mo. Rev. Stat. § 474.160. In some cases other property and money the decedent was involved with can be covered. Clearly if a spouse uses an Elective Share to get 1/2 or 1/3 of decedent's things this may take so much it interferes with other transfers. To avoid a spouse wanting to use the Elective Share most people give over 1/2 of things to any spouse.

CHILD ISSUES

WILL CAN NAME A GUARDIAN OF THE PERSON TO CARE FOR YOUNG CHILD

If a parent dies with a child under age 18 then any other natural or adopted parent (but not a step-parent) almost always automatically gets control of the child's care (including health care, school, and home issues). This won't occur only if the other parent will be unavailable a long time or is proven unfit in court which is rare. But just in case it is later needed (like later both parents die) a Will often names a healthy and willing relative or friend as "Guardian of the Person" to if needed give this care for a young child.

WILL CAN NAME A CONSERVATOR TO MANAGE CHILD'S PROPERTY

Since a child until age 18 can't legally easily control property including money a Will often names a person to be "Conservator" to have the job of managing a young child's property and money. Many states call this a "Guardian of the Estate". This person decides each year how to use property and money on a child's needs (like on school, health care, and living costs) and then usually at age 18 anything left then goes to the child. A person paying things for a child can ask to be paid back. A judge often holds a yearly hearing to review all spending. As a nice 2nd option to avoid work and costs most Wills say an Executor may name a person including themselves as "Custodian" to manage things under the new Uniform Transfers To Minors Act.

MOST WILLS NAME 1 PERSON TO CARE FOR CHILD AND THEIR PROPERTY

This book's Will forms and most parents name the same 1 person to care for a child and also manage a child's property and money. People can change a Will to name different people for the 2 positions, but this is rarely worth it since parents dying is rare, rarely do children get much, a person smart enough to handle a child often can handle money, and naming different people can lead to arguments and even costly lawsuits between people. Will gifts can go to someone named to be a Guardian or Conservator.

PERSON TO HELP A CHILD MUST BE AT LEAST 18

To be a person helping a child in Missouri a person must be at least age 18 but they needn't reside here. But later usually a judge can't think they are unfit to serve, which usually means no serious criminal felony or a history of abuse or fraud. The choice by the last living parent is usually followed. If no Will names a person for a position or they're unavailable a judge can pick someone, but family may argue about who to suggest. Naming 2 people to act at the same time in the same position is rare since 2 persons may argue and any 1 person named should be smart enough to act alone. In rare cases a married couple is named for the same position but there can be problems if they divorce or disagree. Some Wills add a 2nd person to serve if the 1st person named is later not available, like: "or if they are later unable to serve I name _____ to serve"). But most people skip naming a fallback person since it is rarely needed, if a problem is seen a Will can be redone by a person, and a judge can just pick someone if needed.

NAMING PERSONS TO HELP CHILD RARELY MATTERS

A child under 18 having parents die is rare so parents shouldn't worry much about naming people to help. A good U.S. study looked at 72,240 people under age 18 and found only 2014 had lost 1 parent (so 2.78%) and only 97 had lost 2 parents (so a very small 0.13%). *Parent Mortality Census SIPP Paper #288.*

CHAPTER 6
BASIC IDEAS ABOUT HEALTH CARE FORMS

BASIC IDEAS HELP PEOPLE UNDERSTAND CONTROLLING HEALTH CARE

Some ideas help people understand health care forms.

■ By law people controls their own health care by telling medical personnel what they want <u>unless they are "incapacitated"</u> by insufficient ability to a) <u>communicate</u> verbally or by notes, b) be <u>rational</u>, or c) be <u>conscious</u>. Most people keep control of their own care till death or till no big treatment options remain, but some people worry they may be incapacitated a long time so want to do health care forms.

■ Legal documents that help control health care are usually called "Advanced Directives".

■ If an adult 18 or older becomes incapacitated <u>the adult's closest family like spouse or adult child usually can make emergency decisions</u>. But later they usually must then rush to a judge to get further power if no legal document gives them more power over health care.

■ In legal documents a <u>person can be named to have control of health care</u> if needed. This person is often called the "Health Care Agent" or similar.

■ In legal documents people can give <u>written medical instructions that doctors, family, and Agent must obey</u>.

■ Parents even without legal documents usually have power over health care of <u>children under age 18</u>.

■ Some <u>married people</u> do documents to give a spouse power over medical care if they are incapacitated. Some adults give this power to parents. Young people are rarely badly sick so often skip doing these things.

■ Pain relief like pain drugs or comfort care is still given even if documents say to stop or limit other care.

■ <u>Most people only do 1 legal document</u> about health care that often names someone to control health care if needed and has a spot for basic instructions (this is sometimes called a "Health Care Power of Attorney").

■ For the rare times stopping health care seems more likely to matter (like due to extreme illness or old age):

-- most people do nothing special and trust family or Health Care Agent to wisely decide when to stop care (they can weigh many factors like pain, cost, likely difficulty of treatment, beliefs, and chances of recovery);

-- a few people do a serious document to say to stop most health care if <u>later</u> doctors think an incapacitated person has very bad health and more medical care likely won't help (sometimes this is called a "Living Will");

-- a few people do a serious document to say <u>starting immediately</u> to not try most medical care (sometimes this is called a "Do-Not-Resuscitate" if about resuscitation or called a "Physician's Order" if about many treatments).

CHAPTER 7
FORM 1: WILL (STANDARD)

FORM 1 IS A STANDARD WILL THAT IS FLEXIBLE BUT WITHOUT GUARDIANS

Form 1 is a flexible Will that lets a person control many things after their death. This form has no part about a Guardian so is for a person with no child under age 18. A person doing a Will is called a Testator.

THIS FORM IS A WILL WITH SEVERAL PARTS

The form starts with lines for a person to put their name (a full legal name is best but not required) and place of main residence (most put a county but some put a city). The Will is still valid if people later move.

Paragraph 1, "Living Spouse And Children", lets the names of any living spouse and any living children be written (or if there are none skip this or maybe put "none"). This helps show a person is mentally fit and with enough memory to do a Will. Wrongly not listing someone here can let them ask a judge to give them a share or all of a Testator's property and money by claiming they were accidently forgotten.

Paragraph 2, "Gifts", has many spaces to make some specific gifts of particular property or some general gifts like of money. People can delete, copy and paste to add more, or leave blank these gift lines.

Paragraph 3, "Separate Writings", says to follow any separate writings done at a later time apart from the Will that gifts tangible personal property (see earlier part of this book explaining such a writing).

Paragraph 4, "Residue", has a Residue Clause to say any property and money left after earlier Will parts and other transfers is to be distributed in the way a person wrote in the blank parts of this paragraph.

Paragraph 5, "Administration", names a person to be Personal Representative to do things after a person's death (in the past the term Executor was usually used in Missouri for the person doing this).

Paragraph 6, "Miscellaneous", has paragraphs of legal language to help avoid certain legal issues.

Last is a paragraph for Testator to put the date and sign, and a paragraph for 2 witnesses to put the date, sign, and print the addresses they live at.

USUAL RESIDUE CLAUSE HAS 2 PLACES TO NAME PERSONS TO GET THINGS

In a Will "Residue Clause" anything left over after other Will parts is transferred as the clause directs. Many people use a Residue Clause to gift most their things. In this Will form's Residue Clause there is:

1) a 1st space to name 1 or more persons to get the Residue, and if any named here have died before the Will maker then other persons named here in this 1st space take the dead person's share, and

2) a 2nd space to name people to get things if all people named in the 1st space have died, and if any people named in the 2nd space have died their shares go to "lineal descendants" like their children.

People often put in the 1st space a spouse or closest family or friends, and in 2nd space next closest people.

TESTATOR AND 2 WITNESSES WHILE TOGETHER SIGN WILL

This Will after being filled out (except bits intentionally left blank) must be signed by the person doing the Will (the "Testator") in front of at least 2 persons acting as witnesses at least age 18 who then also sign.

LAST WILL AND TESTAMENT

I, _____, of _____, Missouri, do revoke all prior Wills and testamentary documents and do make, publish, and declare this as my Will. I am of sound mind and under no duress or undue influence and acting voluntarily.

1. LIVING SPOUSE AND CHILDREN. To show I am mentally fit and have sufficient memory to do a Will I do say I now have the following living spouse and living children:
_____
_____.

2. GIFTS. I give these gifts in this Will, but to get a gift in this section the recipient must survive me except as otherwise stated below.

I give _____ to _____.

I give _____ to _____.

I give _____ to _____.

I give _____ to _____.

I give _____ to _____.

I give _____ to _____.

I give _____ to _____.

I give _____ to _____.

I give _____ to _____.

I give _____ to _____.

I give _____ to _____.

I give _____ to _____.

I give _____ to _____.

3. SEPARATE WRITINGS. I may do writings separate from this Will to gift tangible personal property as allowed by state law, and all such writings should be followed. But any such writing not found within 90 days of my death is canceled and has no effect. A gift in such a writing to a person who does not survive me is canceled and has no effect. This Will does not revoke any such writings that now exist.

4. RESIDUE. The rest, residue, and remainder of my estate, and anything else, I give:
   a) to _____ who survive me, and with persons just named who survive me taking the share of non-survivors, then if anything remains
   b) to _____ and if any of those just now named do not survive me their part goes to their lineal descendants per stirpes.

5. ADMINISTRATION. I name, nominate, and appoint _____ as Personal Representative including for me, my Will, and my estate.

6. MISCELLANEOUS. The following applies to this Will and generally.
   In this Will no part left unfilled is a mistake including spaces in the residue clause.
   The facts support and I want Missouri state law to apply to this Will and my estate.
   I order that my just debts, funeral and related expenses, and taxes be paid as soon after my death as practical but only those items my Personal Representative chooses to pay.
   Priority of Will gifts of the same type is based on the order they are written.
   The words "give" and "gift" also means a devise, bequest, grant, legacy, or similar.
   I am intentionally not providing by Will or other ways for some family, including I am not providing for some children of mine and also children of a deceased child of mine.
   If a Will gift reasonably mentions survival then survival is an absolute condition and anti-lapse laws or similar provisions have no effect and without survival the gift lapses. Unless a Will gift specifies otherwise if a Will gift goes to multiple recipients if any do not survive me the part to them lapses and instead goes to other surviving recipients.
   No earlier transfer reduces a Will gift unless I usually called it a loan or advancement.
   In this Will any gender or gendered word includes all genders, and the singular includes the plural and vice versa, and "they" can mean a single person or many persons.
   Unless a Will specifically says otherwise a secured debt including a mortgage or lien shall not be paid off including by a Personal Representative or in probate, and a recipient of a Will gift of property takes it subject to debts. Also, no recipient of property who may lose it or who pays to keep it may have my estate or others pay or do exoneration.
   If during my life I disposed of an item in a specific gift then the gift is extinguished.
   I request and authorize any informal, summary, and quick probate or similar action. Any Personal Representative may act independently with no supervision of any court, including independent administration, and with no inventory, appraisal, or other action.
   I give any Personal Representative the a) fullest authority, discretion, and powers allowed by state law, b) power to lease, sell, mortgage, convey, or keep property including real property in a manner and time they deem helpful or proper, and c) authority to settle or pay claims or debts in the time and manner they choose. Any Personal Representative or other fiduciary shall have all powers and authorities conferred by statute or common law in any jurisdiction they may act, including powers and authorities conferred by state law.
   Any Guardian of any type, Conservator, Custodian, or other person managing a minor's

property or money may use or invade the principal and sell property without court action.

If context permits the terms Personal Representative and Executor and Administrator are interchangeable, Conservator and Guardian of the Estate and Guardian of Property and Custodian are interchangeable, and residue and residuary are interchangeable. Any such person may stand in the place of and have all powers like the others named here.

The residue includes lapsed or failed gifts, insurance paid to the estate, digital assets, inheritances owed me, and all I had power of appointment or testamentary disposition over.

Any Personal Representative may access, manage, delete, modify, transfer, and otherwise control any digital accounts and assets I had any interest in or power over.

Any Personal Representative, Executor, Administrator, Guardian of any type like for a person or estate, Conservator, Custodian, and any other fiduciary under this Will or otherwise shall qualify and serve without bond, surety, security, surety bond, or similar.

If evidence does not show it likely a person survived me by 120 hours (5 days) then for this Will and my estate they shall be deemed in all ways as having died before me.

If part of this Will is by law invalid or unenforceable other provisions remain in effect.

Any Personal Representative may at any time transfer money or property of a minor under age 18 to a Custodian to serve under the Missouri Uniform Transfers to Minors Act or similar law anywhere, and may pick a person to be Custodian including themselves.

TESTATOR

IN WITNESS WHEREOF, I declare and publish that this instrument is my Will which I make as Testator and I now voluntarily sign on the ____ day of _____, 20___.

_____
Signature of Testator

WITNESSES

We, the undersigned Witnesses, declared the foregoing instrument was published, declared, and signed by the Testator in our presence to be the Will of the Testator, and we certify that the Testator appeared in all ways to be of sound and disposing mind and memory at the time and over the age of 18 years, and we sign our names hereunto acting to witness the Will at the request and in the presence of the Testator, and in the presence of each other on the ____ day of _____, 20___.

_____   _____
Signature of Witness #1   Address of Witness #1

_____   _____
Signature of Witness #2   Address of Witness #2

CHAPTER 8
FORM 2: WILL (GUARDIAN)

FORM 2 IS A WILL WITH GUARDIAN PART FOR PEOPLE WITH YOUNG CHILD

Form 2 is a Will with a Guardian part to be used by a person with a minor child under age 18.

FORM IS A WILL WITH SEVERAL PARTS INCLUDING A GUARDIAN PART

The form starts with lines for a person to put their name (a full legal name is best but not required) and place of main residence (most put a county but some put a city). The Will is still valid if people later move.

Paragraph 1, "Living Spouse And Children", lets names of any living spouse and any living children be written (or if there are none skip this or maybe put "none"). This helps show a person is mentally fit and with enough memory to do a Will. Wrongly not listing someone here can sometimes cause legal problems.

Paragraph 2, "Gifts", has many spaces to make some specific gifts of particular property or some general gifts like of money. People can delete, copy and paste to add more, or leave blank these gift lines.

Paragraph 3, "Separate Writings", says to follow any separate writings done at a later time apart from the Will that gifts tangible personal property (see earlier part of this book explaining such a writing).

Paragraph 4, "Residue", has a Residue Clause to say any property and money left after earlier Will parts and other transfers is to be distributed in the way a person wrote in the blank parts of this paragraph.

Paragraph 5, "Administration", names a person to be Personal Representative to do things after a person's death (in the past the term Executor was usually used in Missouri for the person doing this).

<u>**Paragraph 6, "Guardian"**, names a person as Guardian to care for minor children under 18 if needed (like if both parents die) and also be Conservator to manage property and money of children.</u>

Paragraph 7, "Miscellaneous", has paragraphs of legal language to help avoid certain legal issues.

Last is a paragraph for Testator to put the date and sign, and a paragraph for 2 witnesses to put the date, sign, and print the addresses they live at.

USUAL RESIDUE CLAUSE HAS 2 PLACES TO NAME PERSONS TO GET THINGS

In a Will "Residue Clause" anything left over after other Will parts is transferred as the clause directs. Many people use a Residue Clause to gift most their things. In this Will form's Residue Clause there is:

1) a 1st space to name 1 or more persons to get the Residue, and if any named here have died before the Will maker then other persons named here in this 1st space take the dead person's share, and

2) a 2nd space to name people to get things if all people named in the 1st space have died, and if any people named in the 2nd space have died their shares go to "lineal descendants" like their children.

People often put in the 1st space a spouse or closest family or friends, and in 2nd space next closest people.

TESTATOR AND 2 WITNESSES WHILE TOGETHER SIGN WILL

This Will after being filled out (except bits intentionally left blank) must be signed by the person doing the Will (the "Testator") in front of at least 2 persons acting as witnesses at least age 18 who then also sign.

LAST WILL AND TESTAMENT

I, _____, of _____, Missouri, do revoke all prior Wills and testamentary documents and do make, publish, and declare this as my Will. I am of sound mind and under no duress or undue influence and acting voluntarily.

1. LIVING SPOUSE AND CHILDREN. To show I am mentally fit and have sufficient memory to do a Will I do say I now have the following living spouse and living children:
_____
_____.

2. GIFTS. I give these gifts in this Will, but to get a gift in this section the recipient must survive me except as otherwise stated below.

I give _____ to _____.

I give _____ to _____.

I give _____ to _____.

I give _____ to _____.

I give _____ to _____.

I give _____ to _____.

I give _____ to _____.

I give _____ to _____.

I give _____ to _____.

3. SEPARATE WRITINGS. I may do writings separate from this Will to gift tangible personal property as allowed by state law, and all such writings should be followed. But any such writing not found within 90 days of my death is canceled and has no effect. A gift in such a writing to a person who does not survive me is canceled and has no effect. This Will does not revoke any such writings that now exist.

4. RESIDUE. The rest, residue, and remainder of my estate, and anything else, I give:
 a) to _____ who survive me, and with persons just named who survive me taking the share of non-survivors, then if anything remains
 b) to _____ and if any of those just now named do not survive me their part goes to their lineal descendants per stirpes.

5. ADMINISTRATION. I name, nominate, and appoint _____
as Personal Representative including for me, my Will, and my estate.

6. GUARDIAN. I name, nominate, and appoint _____
to be Guardian of any minor child of mine and also to have care, authority, custody, and other control of them. I also name this same person to be Conservator for any minor child and also to have care, control, and power over their property, money, and estate.

7. MISCELLANEOUS. The following applies to this Will and generally.

In this Will no part left unfilled is a mistake including spaces in the residue clause.

The facts support and I want Missouri state law to apply to this Will and my estate.

I order that my just debts, funeral and related expenses, and taxes be paid as soon after my death as practical but only those items my Personal Representative chooses to pay.

Priority of Will gifts of the same type is based on the order they are written.

The words "give" and "gift" also means a devise, bequest, grant, legacy, or similar.

I am intentionally not providing by Will or other ways for some family, including I am not providing for some children of mine and also children of a deceased child of mine.

If a Will gift reasonably mentions survival then survival is an absolute condition and anti-lapse laws or similar provisions have no effect and without survival the gift lapses. Unless a Will gift specifies otherwise if a Will gift goes to multiple recipients if any do not survive me the part to them lapses and instead goes to other surviving recipients.

No earlier transfer reduces a Will gift unless I usually called it a loan or advancement.

In this Will any gender or gendered word includes all genders, and the singular includes the plural and vice versa, and "they" can mean a single person or many persons.

Unless a Will specifically says otherwise a secured debt including a mortgage or lien shall not be paid off including by a Personal Representative or in probate, and a recipient of a Will gift of property takes it subject to debts. Also, no recipient of property who may lose it or who pays to keep it may have my estate or others pay or do exoneration.

If during my life I disposed of an item in a specific gift then the gift is extinguished.

I request and authorize any informal, summary, and quick probate or similar action. Any Personal Representative may act independently with no supervision of any court, including independent administration, and with no inventory, appraisal, or other action.

I give any Personal Representative the a) fullest authority, discretion, and powers allowed by state law, b) power to lease, sell, mortgage, convey, or keep property including real property in a manner and time they deem helpful or proper, and c) authority to settle or pay claims or debts in the time and manner they choose. Any Personal Representative or other fiduciary shall have all powers and authorities conferred by statute or common law in any jurisdiction they may act, including powers and authorities conferred by state law.

Any Guardian of any type, Conservator, Custodian, or other person managing a minor's property or money may use or invade the principal and sell property without court action.

5. ADMINISTRATION. I name, nominate, and appoint _____
as Personal Representative including for me, my Will, and my estate.

6. GUARDIAN. I name, nominate, and appoint _____
to be Guardian of any minor child of mine and also to have care, authority, custody, and other control of them. I also name this same person to be Conservator for any minor child and also to have care, control, and power over their property, money, and estate.

7. MISCELLANEOUS. The following applies to this Will and generally.

In this Will no part left unfilled is a mistake including spaces in the residue clause.

The facts support and I want Missouri state law to apply to this Will and my estate.

I order that my just debts, funeral and related expenses, and taxes be paid as soon after my death as practical but only those items my Personal Representative chooses to pay.

Priority of Will gifts of the same type is based on the order they are written.

The words "give" and "gift" also means a devise, bequest, grant, legacy, or similar.

I am intentionally not providing by Will or other ways for some family, including I am not providing for some children of mine and also children of a deceased child of mine.

If a Will gift reasonably mentions survival then survival is an absolute condition and anti-lapse laws or similar provisions have no effect and without survival the gift lapses. Unless a Will gift specifies otherwise if a Will gift goes to multiple recipients if any do not survive me the part to them lapses and instead goes to other surviving recipients.

No earlier transfer reduces a Will gift unless I usually called it a loan or advancement.

In this Will any gender or gendered word includes all genders, and the singular includes the plural and vice versa, and "they" can mean a single person or many persons.

Unless a Will specifically says otherwise a secured debt including a mortgage or lien shall not be paid off including by a Personal Representative or in probate, and a recipient of a Will gift of property takes it subject to debts. Also, no recipient of property who may lose it or who pays to keep it may have my estate or others pay or do exoneration.

If during my life I disposed of an item in a specific gift then the gift is extinguished.

I request and authorize any informal, summary, and quick probate or similar action. Any Personal Representative may act independently with no supervision of any court, including independent administration, and with no inventory, appraisal, or other action.

I give any Personal Representative the a) fullest authority, discretion, and powers allowed by state law, b) power to lease, sell, mortgage, convey, or keep property including real property in a manner and time they deem helpful or proper, and c) authority to settle or pay claims or debts in the time and manner they choose. Any Personal Representative or other fiduciary shall have all powers and authorities conferred by statute or common law in any jurisdiction they may act, including powers and authorities conferred by state law.

Any Guardian of any type, Conservator, Custodian, or other person managing a minor's property or money may use or invade the principal and sell property without court action.

If context permits the terms Personal Representative and Executor and Administrator are interchangeable, Conservator and Guardian of the Estate and Guardian of Property and Custodian are interchangeable, and residue and residuary are interchangeable. Any such person may stand in the place of and have all powers like the others named here.

The residue includes lapsed or failed gifts, insurance paid to the estate, digital assets, inheritances owed me, and all I had power of appointment or testamentary disposition over.

Any Personal Representative may access, manage, delete, modify, transfer, and otherwise control any digital accounts and assets I had any interest in or power over.

Any Personal Representative, Executor, Administrator, Guardian of any type like for a person or estate, Conservator, Custodian, and any other fiduciary under this Will or otherwise shall qualify and serve without bond, surety, security, surety bond, or similar.

If evidence does not show it likely a person survived me by 120 hours (5 days) then for this Will and my estate they shall be deemed in all ways as having died before me.

If part of this Will is by law invalid or unenforceable other provisions remain in effect.

Any Personal Representative may at any time transfer money or property of a minor under age 18 to a Custodian to serve under the Missouri Uniform Transfers to Minors Act or similar law anywhere, and may pick a person to be Custodian including themselves.

TESTATOR

IN WITNESS WHEREOF, I declare and publish that this instrument is my Will which I make as Testator and I now voluntarily sign on the ____ day of _____, 20___.

_____
Signature of Testator

WITNESSES

We, the undersigned Witnesses, declared the foregoing instrument was published, declared, and signed by the Testator in our presence to be the Will of the Testator, and we certify that the Testator appeared in all ways to be of sound and disposing mind and memory at the time and over the age of 18 years, and we sign our names hereunto acting to witness the Will at the request and in the presence of the Testator, and in the presence of each other on the ____ day of _____, 20___.

_____   _____
Signature of Witness #1   Address of Witness #1

_____   _____
Signature of Witness #2   Address of Witness #2

CHAPTER 9
FORM 3: SELF-PROVING AFFIDAVIT

FORM CAN BE DONE TO HELP WITH THE WORK OF USING A WILL LATER

This form is optional but can be done with a Will or anytime afterward to help with the legal work that is involved in later using a Will after a death.

FORM HELPS SHOW A WILL WAS PROPERLY SIGNED

The Self-Proving Affidavit helps "prove" a Will was signed properly. If this form isn't done then after a death a little more work is needed to get evidence from either witnesses to the Will signing, persons familiar with the signatures of people, or a handwriting expert. Without the Self-Proving Affidavit there is a bit more legal risk a Will won't be followed later. But of people doing Wills about half skip a Self-Proving Affidavit mostly due to hassle of finding a notary on top of 2 witnesses each time a Will is done or re-done, and since it mostly just saves a little later work of people who are happy to do work to get what the Will gives them.

FORM IS DONE BY TESTATOR AND 2 WITNESSES SIGNING BEFORE NOTARY

For this form to be valid a person who is a notary (also called a "notary public") must see the Testator and 2 witnesses sign this form and then the notary notarizes the form. A notary can be found and asked to help at a bank, insurance agent, government office, or by first using a phonebook. This form is often done a few minutes after a Will is signed but it also can be done much later (even years later) when everyone can meet with a notary. But this form can't legally be done before a Will is done. This form when done is often kept paper-clipped to the Will it supports.

SELF-PROVING AFFIDAVIT

THE STATE OF MISSOURI)
) ss.
COUNTY OF _____)

We, _____, _____, and _____, the Testator and the Witnesses, respectively, whose names are signed to the attached or foregoing instrument, being first duly sworn, do hereby declare to the undersigned authority that the Testator signed and executed the instrument as the Will of Testator and that the Testator had signed willingly, and that the Testator executed it as the Testator's free and voluntary act for the purposes therein expressed, and each of the Witnesses, in the presence and hearing of the Testator, signed the Will acting as witness and that to the best of each of the Witness' knowledge the Testator was at the time 18 years of age or older, of sound mind, and under no constraint or undue influence.

                _____
                Testator

_____   _____
Witness   Witness

STATE OF MISSOURI)
) ss.
CITY OF _____)

The foregoing instrument was acknowledged before me this ____ day of _____, 20_____, by _____, the Testator and _____ and _____, the Witnesses.

_____
Notary Public

CHAPTER 10
FORM 4: TANGIBLE PERSONAL PROPERTY MEMORANDUM

FORM LETS MORE GIFTS TO OCCUR AFTER DEATH BE EASILY WRITTEN OUT

This form lets more gifts to occur after death be easily written, but it can only cover tangible personal property (this is most household items, vehicles, and jewelry). Many people call this a memo or list form.

FORM GIVES EASY AND QUICK WAY TO WRITE MORE GIFTS OF PROPERTY

This form lets people write out gifts of property to occur after death without any need to redo a full Will or somehow modify it. To use this form a valid Will must have been done saying these writings can be used, and most Wills in Missouri say this (including Wills in this book). If this form and a Will cover the same item then legally the Will later controls what happens. If 2 of these forms cover the same item then the more recently done page controls. People can modify or add to an existing form page if they then put a new date and signature. Doing gifts by putting stickers or notes on items is not recommended or legal, and it is best to use this form. To avoid delay the form says to ignore the form if it isn't found within 90 days of a death.

FORM CAN ONLY GIFT TANGIBLE PERSONAL PROPERTY

By law the form can only gift "tangible personal property". This is property that is tangible (touchable), so not accounts or moneys or investments where ownership involves paperwork or a bank or other entity. This is property that is personal property, so not real property (land or buildings) and not fixtures (anything buried or tied to land) and not money. The form also can't gift any money, whether coin or paper currency, and no matter how old or foreign. The form also can't gift property used in a trade or business (including most small home businesses). Improper property written in the form is later just ignored. This form is often used to gift clothes, furniture, cars, boats, antiques, electronics, appliances, tools, building supplies, art, and jewelry.

It may help to see the Missouri law allowing the form, which says:

"**Mo. Rev. Stat. § 74.333. Will may provide for disposal of personal property by separate list. —**

A will may refer to a written statement or list to dispose of items of tangible personal property not otherwise specifically disposed of by the will, other than money, evidences of indebtedness, documents of title, securities, and property used in trade or business.

To be admissible under this section as evidence of the intended disposition, the writing must either be in the handwriting of the testator or be signed by the testator, must be dated and must describe the items and the devisees with reasonable certainty.

The writing may:
  (1) Be referred to as one to be in existence at the time of the testator's death;
  (2) Be prepared before or after the execution of the will;
  (3) Be altered by the testator after its preparation; and
  (4) Be a writing which has no significance apart from its effect upon the dispositions made by the will."

TO COMPLETE THE FORM A PERSON SIGNS AND DATES IT

The form must be signed and usually dated, and no witnesses are needed. Pages of this form are often kept by a Will. To cancel this form it can be destroyed, crossed out, or just thrown away so it isn't found later.

TANGIBLE PERSONAL PROPERTY LIST

In this writing are gifts of tangible personal property to occur at my death, but this writing if not found by someone within 90 days of my death is canceled.

I may do many pages of these writings which should all be seen as one document. If there are conflicts among such writings the provisions of the more recent writing will revoke the inconsistent provisions of a prior writing.

If a person getting a gift below does not survive me such gift is void and canceled.

DESCRIPTION OF PROPERTY	NAME OF PERSONS TO GET PROPERTY
_____	to _____
_____	to _____
_____	to _____
_____	to _____
_____	to _____
_____	to _____
_____	to _____
_____	to _____
_____	to _____
_____	to _____
_____	to _____
_____	to _____
_____	to _____
_____	to _____
_____	to _____
_____	to _____
_____	to _____
_____	to _____

DATE:_____   SIGNED:_____

CHAPTER 11
FORM 5: DURABLE POWER OF ATTORNEY FOR HEALTH CARE AND/OR HEALTH CARE DIRECTIVE

IN FORM CAN NAME AGENT AND/OR LET DOCTORS STOP CARE

This form has 2 parts which can 1) name Agent to control health care if needed, and 2) say if doctors should stop care later. Letting care be stopped later is usually done only by the sickest or oldest people. This long form is too hard for paramedics or similar personnel to read fast and this form is mostly for inside hospitals or similar places. The form shown here for educational purposes is based on the Missouri State Bar form, and this form has become the main standard form used in Missouri.

IN FIRST PART OF FORM A PERSON CAN BE NAMED "AGENT"

The first part of form, "Durable Power Of Attorney" part, lets a person name someone as "Agent" to get power to make medical decisions if the person is later incapacitated (if they can't communicate, be rational, or be awake enough to control care by themselves). This person is sometimes called the "Attorney-in-Fact". Often named is a spouse, adult child, relative, or friend. Naming a family member as Agent can avoid their need to rush to see judge to get power in an emergency. People associated with a place giving health care shouldn't be made Agent like a doctor or nurse unless they are family. There is a spot to name a second person to act if the first person doesn't, but most skip this as rarely needed. Instructions can also be written which the Agent and family legally must follow, but many people skip this since it is hard to write clear instructions for all situations and most people trust their Agent and family to wisely handle things.

IN SECOND PART A "LIVING WILL" SAYS DOCTORS LATER CAN STOP CARE

The second part of form, "Living Will Directive" part, lets a person say health care should stop if later the doctors think person is incapacitated and is in very bad health and more health care likely won't help. The form has options about later stopping care, like what treatments to stop and how bad must a person's health be. Many people skip this part since it is stressful to decide and they trust their Agent or family.

PERSON SIGNING FORM MAY NEED NOTARY AND MAY NEED 2 WITNESSES

People can do either or both parts of this form. If the first part was done to name an Agent then the person doing the form must sign in front of a notary. If the second part, Living Will Directive, was done about stopping care then the person must sign in front of 2 witnesses. If both parts of the form are done then both a notary and 2 witnesses are needed. It is suggested that witnesses be at least age 18, not named Agent in the form, and not be related to a person doing the form. Once it is completed the form usually should be shown to all places that may give care to put into a person's medical file and then follow. A person also often gives the form to Agent or family. To cancel the form a person tells any Agent and maybe places which saw the form. Note, item 6 in the form can give control over funeral, cremation, and burial of the body after death (the "sepulcher" right) if a person doesn't want family to control this like usual.

DURABLE POWER OF ATTORNEY FOR HEALTH CARE AND/OR HEALTH CARE DIRECTIVE

(Print full name here) _____

(Address, City, State, Zip) _____

PART I. DURABLE POWER OF ATTORNEY FOR HEALTH CARE
(If you DO NOT WISH to name someone to serve as your decision-making Agent, mark an "X" through Part I on pages 1 & 2 and continue on to Part II.)

1. **Selection of Agent.** I, _____, currently a resident of _____ County, Missouri, appoint the following person as my true and lawful attorney-in-fact ("Agent"):

   Name: _____

   Address: _____

   _____

   Phone(s): 1st _____ 2nd _____

2. **Alternate Agent.** If my Agent resigns or is not able or available to make health care decisions for me, or if an Agent named by me is divorced from me or is my spouse and legally separated from me, I appoint the following persons in the order named below to serve as my alternate Agent and to have the same powers as my Agent:

First Alternate Agent: **Second Alternate Agent:**

Name: _____   Name: _____

Address: _____   Address: _____

_____   _____

Phone(s): 1st _____   Phone(s): 1st _____

2nd _____   2nd _____

3. **Durability.** This is a Durable Power of Attorney, and the authority of my Agent, when effective, shall not terminate or be void or voidable if I am or become disabled or incapacitated or in the event of later uncertainty as to whether I am dead or alive.

4. **Effective Date as to Health Care Decision Making.** This Durable Power of Attorney is effective as to health care decision making when I am incapacitated and unable to make and communicate a health care decision as certified by *(check one of the following boxes):* ☐ one physician **OR** ☐ two physicians.

5. **Agent's Powers.** I grant to my Agent full authority as to health care decision making to:

   A. Give consent to, prohibit, or withdraw any type of health care, long-term care, hospice or palliative care, medical care, treatment, or procedure, either in my residence or a facility outside of my residence, even if my death may result, including, but not limited to, an out of hospital do-not-resuscitate order, with the following specific authorization *(initial one of the following boxes to indicate your choice):*

   [Initials]   I wish to AUTHORIZE my Agent to direct a health care provider to withhold or withdraw artificially supplied nutrition and hydration (including tube feeding of food and water);

   [Initials]   OR I DO NOT AUTHORIZE my Agent to direct a health care provider to withhold or withdraw artificially supplied nutrition and hydration (including tube feeding of food and water);

   B. Make all necessary arrangements for health care services on my behalf and to hire and fire medical personnel responsible for my care;

Part I - After completed, detach, make copies and give to your health care providers.
Durable Power of Attorney for Health Care and/or Health Care Directive

C. Move me into, or out of, any health care or assisted living/residential care facility or my home (even if against medical advice) to obtain compliance with the decisions of my Agent;

D. Take any other action necessary to do what I authorize here, including, but not limited to, granting any waiver or release from liability required by any health care provider and taking any legal action at the expense of my estate to enforce this Durable Power of Attorney for Health Care;

E. Receive information regarding my health care, obtain copies of and review my medical records, consent to the disclosure of my medical records, and act as my "personal representative" as defined in the regulations [45 C.F.R. 164.502(g)] enacted pursuant to the Health Insurance Portability and Accountability Act of 1996 ("HIPAA");

6. **Effective Date as to Other Authority.** In addition to the powers set forth above, I authorize effective upon my signature and without the need for a physician's certification of incapacity that my Agent be authorized to have one or more of the following powers *(initial your desired choices):*

____Initials____ Determine what happens to my body after my death (authority for right of sepulcher);

____Initials____ Give consent after my death to an autopsy or postmortem examination of my remains;

____Initials____ Delegate health care decision-making power to another person ("Delegee") as selected by my Agent, and the Delegee shall be identified in writing by my Agent;

With respect to anatomical gifts of my body or any part (i.e., organs or tissues), please initial your desired choice below:

____Initials____ **AUTHORIZATION OF ANATOMICAL GIFTS.** I wish to AUTHORIZE my Agent to make an anatomical gift of my body or part (organ or tissue).

My donations are for the following purposes: (check one)	GIFT SPECIFICATIONS: (check one) I would like to donate
☐ Transplantation ☐ Therapy ☐ Research ☐ Education ☐ All the above	☐ Any needed organs and tissues, as allowed by law. ☐ Any needed organs and tissues as allowed by law, with the following restrictions:

____Initials____ **PROHIBITION OF ANATOMICAL GIFTS.** I DO NOT AUTHORIZE my Agent to make an anatomical gift of my body or any part (organ or tissue).

7. **Agent's Financial Liability and Compensation.** My Agent, acting under this Durable Power of Attorney for Health Care, will incur no personal financial liability. My Agent shall not be entitled to compensation for services performed under this Durable Power of Attorney for Health Care, but my Agent shall be entitled to reimbursement for all reasonable expenses incurred as a result of carrying out any provisions hereof.

PART II. HEALTH CARE DIRECTIVE

(If you *DO NOT WISH* to make a health care directive but only wish to have an Agent make your decisions without the directive, be sure that you have completed Part I on pages 1 & 2, mark an "X" through Part II on pages 2 & 3 and continue to Part III.)

1. I make this HEALTH CARE DIRECTIVE ("Directive") to exercise my right to determine the course of my health care and to provide clear and convincing proof of my choices and instructions about my treatment.

2. If I am persistently unconscious or there is no reasonable expectation of my recovery from a seriously incapacitating or terminal illness or condition, I direct that all of the life-prolonging procedures that I have initialed below be withheld or withdrawn.

__Initials__ artificially supplied nutrition and hydration (including tube feeding of food and water)

__Initials__ surgery or other invasive procedures __Initials__ heart-lung resuscitation (CPR)

__Initials__ antibiotics __Initials__ dialysis

__Initials__ mechanical ventilator (respirator) __Initials__ chemotherapy

__Initials__ radiation therapy

__Initials__ other procedures specified by me (insert) _____

__Initials__ all other "life-prolonging" medical or surgical procedures that are merely intended to keep me alive without reasonable hope of improving my condition or curing my illness or injury

3. However, if my physician believes that any life-prolonging procedure may lead to a recovery significant to me as communicated by me or my Agent to my physician, then I direct my physician to try the treatment for a reasonable period of time. If it does not cause my condition to improve, I direct the treatment to be withdrawn even if it shortens my life. I also direct that I be given medical treatment to relieve pain or to provide comfort, even if such treatment might shorten my life, suppress my appetite or my breathing, or be habit-forming.

4. If I have already consented to be on the Missouri organ and tissue donor registry or my Agent has authorized the donation of my organs or tissues, I realize it may be necessary to maintain my body artificially after my death until my organs or tissues can be removed.

IF I HAVE NOT DESIGNATED AN AGENT IN THE DURABLE POWER OF ATTORNEY, PART II OF THIS DOCUMENT IS MEANT TO BE IN FULL FORCE AND EFFECT AS MY HEALTH CARE DIRECTIVE.

PART III. GENERAL PROVISIONS INCLUDED IN THE DURABLE POWER OF ATTORNEY FOR HEALTH CARE AND HEALTH CARE DIRECTIVE

1. **Relationship Between Durable Power of Attorney for Health Care and Health Care Directive.** If I have executed both the Durable Power of Attorney for Health Care and Health Care Directive, I encourage my Agent to:

   A. First, follow my choices as expressed in the above Directive or otherwise from knowing me or having had various discussions with me about making decisions regarding life-prolonging procedures.

   B. Second, if my Agent does not know my choices for the specific decision at hand, but my Agent has evidence of my preferences, my Agent can determine how I would decide. My Agent should consider my values, religious beliefs, past decisions, and past statements. The aim is to choose as I would choose, *even if it is not what my Agent would choose for himself or herself.*

C. Third, if my Agent has little or no knowledge of choices I would make, then my Agent and the physicians will have to make a decision based on what a reasonable person in the same situation would decide. I have confidence in my Agent's ability to make decisions in my best interest if my Agent does not have enough information to follow my preferences.

D. Finally, if the Durable Power of Attorney for Health Care is determined to be ineffective, or if my Agent is not able to serve, the Health Care Directive is intended to be used on its own as firm instructions to my health care providers regarding life-prolonging procedures.

2. Protection of Third Parties Who Rely on My Agent. No person who relies in good faith upon any representations by my Agent or Alternate Agent shall be liable to me, my estate, my heirs or assigns, for recognizing the Agent's authority.

3. Revocation of Prior Durable Power of Attorney for Health Care or Health Care Directive. I revoke any prior living will, declaration or health care directive executed by me. If I have appointed an Agent in a prior durable power of attorney, I revoke any prior health care durable power of attorney or any health care terms contained in that other durable power of attorney and intend that this Durable Power for Attorney for Health Care (if completed) and this Health Care Directive (if completed) replace or supplant earlier documents or provisions of earlier documents.

4. Validity. This document is intended to be valid in any jurisdiction in which it is presented. The provisions of this document are separable, so that the invalidity of one or more provisions shall not affect any others. A copy of this document shall be as valid as the original.

IF YOU HAVE COMPLETED THE ENTIRE DOCUMENT OR ONLY THE DIRECTIVE (PART II), YOU MUST SIGN THIS DOCUMENT IN THE PRESENCE OF TWO WITNESSES.

IN WITNESS WHEREOF, I signed this document on _____(month, date),_____(year).

_____
Signature
Printed Name: _____

TWO WITNESSES:

The person who signed this document is of sound mind and voluntarily signed this document in our presence. Each of the undersigned witnesses is at least eighteen years of age.

Signature _____ Signature _____
Print Name _____ Print Name _____
Address _____ Address _____
_____ _____

NOTARY ACKNOWLEDGEMENT
(Only required if Part I or entire document completed.)

STATE OF MISSOURI)
) SS
COUNTY OF _____)

On this _____ day of _____ (month), _____ (year), before me personally appeared _____ _____, to me known to be the person described in and who executed the foregoing instrument and acknowledged that he/she executed the same as his/her free act and deed.

IN WITNESS WHEREOF, I have hereunto set my hand and affixed my official seal in the County or City and state aforementioned, on the day and year first above written.

_____

_____, Notary Public
(Name Printed)

CHAPTER 12
FORM 6: DO NOT RESUSCITATE

DOES SERIOUS ACT OF SAYING IMMEDIATELY NO LONGER GIVE MOST CARE

This chapter actually has 2 forms which are similar and do serious act of saying to immediately no longer give most or certain health care. Doing this is serious and usually only done by the sickest or oldest people. Both forms are often called the "Do Not Resuscitate" or "DNR" form. Both forms are the official state forms. Both forms are short and usually will be followed by paramedics and similar personnel even if in a hurry. A person's doctor usually has copies of these forms on special colored paper and will help fill these out.

FIRST FORM SAYS TO IMMEDIATELY NOT GIVE MANY KINDS OF CARE

This chapter's first form, the "Transportable Physician Orders For Patient Preferences" form (also called the "T.P.O.P.P." form) says to immediately not give most or certain health care. This form often says to immediately no longer give antibiotics, artificial feeding, and C.P.R. This form is short so it can be read fast and followed by those in a hurry like paramedics, but this form is often used by people in a health care facility. Even if the form is done a person can still go get pain medication or other comfort care including by calling for an ambulance. A person is usually free to cancel this form by telling a doctor or paramedic to give care. The T.P.O.P.P. form has become the main form used to say to immediately not give care, and other forms like this chapter's second form are used less. The state of Kansas also uses the same T.P.O.P.P. form. This form is often called the P.O.L.S.T. form especially when used by physicians in other states.

SECOND FORM SAYS TO IMMEDIATELY NOT TRY RESUSCITATION

This chapter's second form, the "Outside The Hospital Do-Not-Resuscitate form", says to immediately not give any resuscitation, which is trying to restart or help breathing or the heart. Resuscitation usually also covers cardio-pulmonary resuscitation (C.P.R.), defibrillation (electric shocks), and machine or tube breathing. This form is short so it can be read fast and followed by those in a hurry like paramedics. Even if this form has been done a person can still go, including by ambulance, to get pain medication and other comfort care. A person is usually free to override this form, like by telling a doctors or paramedics to now give all care. There is a "wallet card" that a doctor and the person both sign, and often this is kept so it is visible and will be seen by paramedics. Some people may wear a special DNR bracelet specially made for Missouri that doctors can help order.

FORM IS SIGNED BY DOCTOR AND PATIENT

A person's doctor usually has copies of the forms on special colored paper and will help fill these out. To be valid form either of these forms must be signed by a person's doctor or similar health professional, and by the person doing the form or their representative (like someone named Agent in the Durable Power Of Attorney For Health Care). Once the form is done people usually people show it to all places that may give care to add it to medical files to follow. Usually the person also keeps a copy of the form by their bed, on their refrigerator, or on or near their body to show to paramedics or others who may try to give care.

FORM SHALL ACCOMPANY PERSON WHEN TRANSFERRED OR DISCHARGED

Kansas – Missouri Transportable Physician Orders for Patient Preferences (TPOPP/POLST)

This Medical Order set is based on the patient's current medical condition and preferences. Any section not completed indicates default treatment for that section. The original form need not be present at the time of emergency. A copied, faxed or electronic version of this form is valid.

Last Name:	First Name, MI:	
Date of Birth:	Last 4 SSN or Patient ID#:	

A. CHECK ONE
CARDIOPULMONARY RESUSCITATION (CPR): Person has no pulse and is not breathing. If patient is not in cardiopulmonary arrest, follow orders in B and C.

- ☐ **Attempt Resuscitation/CPR** *(Selecting CPR in Section A requires selecting Full Treatment in Section B)*
- ☐ **Do Not Attempt Resuscitation** *(DNAR/no CPR/Allow Natural Death)*

B. CHECK ONE
INITIAL TREATMENT ORDERS: Follow these orders if patient has a pulse and/or is breathing.

Reassess and discuss treatments with patient and/or representative regularly to ensure patients care goals are met.

- ☐ **Full Treatments (required if CPR chosen in Section A).** GOAL: Attempt to sustain life by all medically effective means. Provide appropriate medical treatments as indicated in an attempt to prolong life, including intubation, advanced airway interventions, mechanical ventilation, and defibrillation/cardioversion, including intensive care.
- ☐ **Selective Treatments.** GOAL: Attempt to restore functions while avoiding intensive care and resuscitation efforts (i.e., ventilator, defibrillation, and cardioversion). May use non-invasive positive airway pressure, antibiotics and IV fluids as indicated. Avoid intensive care. Transfer to hospital if treatment needs cannot be met in current location.
- ☐ **Comfort-focused Treatments.** GOAL: Attempt to maximize comfort through symptom management only; allow natural death. Use oxygen, suction and manual treatment of airway obstruction as needed for comfort. Avoid treatments listed in full or selective treatments unless consistent with comfort goal. Transfer to hospital if comfort cannot be achieved in current setting.

C. CHECK ONE
MEDICALLY ADMINISTERED NUTRITION: Offer food by mouth if desired by patient, is safe and tolerated.

- ☐ Provide feeding through new or existing surgically-placed tubes
- ☐ Trial period for medically assisted nutrition but no surgically-placed tubes
- ☐ No medically assisted means of nutrition desired
- ☐ Not discussed or no decision made

D.
ADDITIONAL ORDERS OR INSTRUCTIONS FOR SECTIONS B AND C: Includes e.g., time trials, blood products, and other orders. [EMS Protocols may limit emergency responder ability to act on orders in this section.]

E. CHECK ALL THAT APPLY
INFORMATION AND SIGNATURES (E-Signed documents are valid)

Discussed with:
- ☐ Patient
- ☐ Agent/DPOA Health Care
- ☐ Parent of minor
- ☐ Legal guardian
- ☐ Patient Representative
- ☐ Other *(specify)*: _____

Signature of patient or recognized decision maker (all fields required): By signing this form, the patient/recognized decision maker voluntarily acknowledges that this treatment order is consistent with the known desires and/or best interest of the patient.

Print name: EDUCATIONAL PURPOSES ONLY	Signature: FOR EDUCATIONAL PURPOSES ONLY	The most recently completed valid TPOPP/POLST form supersedes all previously completed TPOPP/POLST forms.
Address:	Relationship:	Phone:

Signature of authorized healthcare provider (all fields required): My signature below indicates to the best of my knowledge that these orders are consistent with the person's medical condition and preferences. (verbal orders are acceptable with follow up signature)

Print name of authorized provider and/or Physician: FOR EDUCATIONAL PURPOSEsS ONLY	Phone:
Signature of authorized provider: FOR EDUCTIONAL PURPOSES ONLY	Date:

HIPAA PERMITS DISCLOSURE TO HEALTH CARE PROFESSIONALS AND PROXY DECISION MAKERS AS NECESSARY FOR TREATMENT

© Center For Practical Bioethics, 1111 Main, Suite 500 (Harzfeld Building), Kansas City, MO 64105 | 816-221-1100   2021

Kansas-Missouri TPOPP
practicalbioethics.org

FORM SHALL ACCOMPANY PERSON WHEN TRANSFERRED OR DISCHARGED

Patient Last Name:	First Name, MI:	DOB:	Last 4 SSN/Patient ID#:

ADVANCE CARE DIRECTIVES & EMERGENCY CONTACTS

Review of Advance Directives (Check all that apply)

- ☐ Healthcare Directive (Living Will)
- ☐ Other Instructions or Documents
- ☐ Advance Directives Unavailable
- ☐ No Advance Directives Exist
- ☐ Appointment of Durable Power of Attorney for Health Care (Name): _____ (Phone): _____

Patient's Emergency Contact (if other than person signing form) and Provider(s)

Full Name: _____ Phone (voice __ text __): _____

Primary Care Provider Name: _____ Phone: _____
Hospice Care Agency (If Applicable) Name: _____ Phone: _____

Health Care Providers and Others Assisting with Form Preparation Process (Check all that apply)

- ☐ Social Worker
- ☐ Nurse
- ☐ Clergy
- ☐ Palliative Care Provider
- ☐ Health Care Agent
- ☐ Parent of Minor
- ☐ Family Member
- ☐ "Person of Care and Concern"
- ☐ Patient Advocate
- ☐ Legal Guardian
- ☐ Other: _____

Instructions for Completing TPOPP/POLST

- Completing a TPOPP/POLST form is always voluntary. TPOPP/POLST is a useful tool for the understanding of and implementation of physicians' orders that are reflective of the current medical condition and preferences of a patient. The orders are to be respected by all receiving providers in compliance with institutional policy. On admission to the hospital setting, a physician who will issue appropriate orders for that inpatient setting will assess the patient.
- TPOPP/POLST is a physician order set and as such does not replace Advance Directives but should serve to clarify them.
- TPOPP/POLST must be completed by a health care provider based on patient preferences and medical indications. Upon completion it must be signed by a physician, APRN, or PA in compliance with state law, regulation, and scope of practice; and by patient (or representative) to be valid.
- Photocopies and Faxes of signed TPOPP/POLST forms are valid. Use of original form is strongly encouraged. A copy shall be retained in patient's medical record and accompany the patient to all settings.

Using TPOPP/POLST

(Any incomplete section of TPOPP/POLST implies full treatment for that section).

- **SECTION A:**
  - If found pulseless and not breathing, no defibrillator (including automated external defibrillators) or chest compressions should be used on a person if "Do Not Attempt Resuscitation" is selected.
- **SECTION B:**
  - When comfort cannot be achieved in the current setting, the person, including someone with "Comfort-focused Treatments" should be transferred to a setting able to provide comfort (e.g., treatment of a hip fracture).
  - Non-invasive positive airway pressure includes continuous positive airway pressure (CPAP), bi-level positive airway pressure (BiPAP), and bag valve mask (BVM) assisted respirations.

Reviewing TPOPP/POLST

- TPOPP/POLST form should be reviewed when:
  - The person is transferred from one care setting or care level to another, or
  - There is a substantial change in the person's health status, or
  - The person's treatment preferences change, or
  - The care provider changes.

Modifying and Voiding TPOPP/POLST

- A patient with capacity can, at any time, request alternative treatment or revoke a TPOPP/POLST by any means that indicates intent to revoke. It is recommended that revocation be documented by drawing a line through Sections A through D, writing "VOID" in large letters, and signing and dating.
- A legally recognized decision-maker may request to modify the orders, in collaboration with the physician/APRN/PA, based on the known desires of the patient or, if unknown, the patient's best interests.

For information, clinical guidance resources or to obtain more forms, contact: TPOPP@practicalbioethics.org

HIPAA PERMITS DISCLOSURE TO HEALTH CARE PROFESSIONALS AND PROXY DECISION MAKERS AS NECESSARY FOR TREATMENT

© Center For Practical Bioethics, 1111 Main, Suite 500 (Harzfeld Building), Kansas City, MO 64105 | 816-221-1100   2021   Kansas-Missouri TPOPP practicalbioethics.org

PAGE INTENTIONALLY LEFT BLANK

OUTSIDE THE HOSPITAL DO-NOT-RESUSCITATE (OHDNR) ORDER

I, _____, authorize emergency medical services personnel to
       (name)
withhold or withdraw cardiopulmonary resuscitation from me in the event I suffer cardiac or respiratory arrest. Cardiac arrest means my heart stops beating and respiratory arrest means I stop breathing.

I understand that in the event that I suffer cardiac or respiratory arrest, this OHDNR order will take effect and no medical procedure to restart breathing or heart functioning will be instituted.

I understand this decision will **not** prevent me from obtaining other emergency medical care and medical interventions, such as intravenous fluids, oxygen or therapies other than cardiopulmonary resuscitation such as those deemed necessary to provide comfort care or to alleviate pain by any health care provider (e.g. paramedics) and/or medical care directed by a physician prior to my death.

I understand I may revoke this order at any time.

I give permission for this OHDNR order to be given to outside the hospital care providers (e.g. paramedics), doctors, nurses, or other health care personnel as necessary to implement this order.

I hereby agree to the "Outside The Hospital Do-Not-Resuscitate" (OHDNR) Order.

Patient – Printed or Typed Name	Date
Patient's Signature or Patient Representative's Signature	Date

REVOCATION PROVISION

I hereby revoke the above declaration.

Patient's Signature or Patient Representative's Signature	Date

I AUTHORIZE EMERGENCY MEDICAL SERVICES PERSONNEL TO WITHHOLD OR WITHDRAW CARDIOPULMONARY RESUSCITATION FROM THE PATIENT IN THE EVENT OF CARDIAC OR RESPIRATORY ARREST.

I affirm this order is the expressed wish of the patient/patient's representative, medically appropriate and documented in the patient's permanent medical record.

Attending Physician's Signature **(Mandatory)**	Date
Attending Physician – Printed or Typed Name	Attending Physician's License No.	Attending Physician's Telephone No.
Address – Printed or Typed		Facility or Agency Name

THIS OHDNR ORDER SHALL REMAIN WITH THE PATIENT WHEN TRANSFERRED OUTSIDE THE HEALTH CARE FACILITY.

Emergency Medical Services personnel shall not comply with an outside the hospital do-not-resuscitate order when the patient or the patient's representative expresses to such personnel in any manner, before or after the onset of a cardiac or respiratory arrest, the desire to be resuscitated or if the patient is or is believed to be pregnant.

Statutory citation 190.600-190.621 RSMo
9/07

Outside the Hospital Do-Not-Resuscitate Identification Card

Patient's Full Name_____

I affirm that I have authorized an Outside the Hospital Do-Not-Resuscitate Order for this patient and have documented the grounds for the order in this patient's medical file.

Attending Physician Signature_____

Attending Physician (print)_____

Address_____**Phone**_____

Date_____

I, _____,
(name)

authorize emergency medical services personnel to withhold or withdraw cardiopulmonary resuscitation from me in the event I suffer cardiac or respiratory arrest.

I understand this means that if my heart stops beating or I stop breathing, no medical procedure to restart heart function or breathing will be instituted.

I understand that I may revoke this order at anytime.

Patient or Patient's Representative
Signature_____
Date_____

CHAPTER 13
FORM 7: DURABLE GENERAL POWER OF ATTORNEY

FORM LETS PERSON GIVE POWER OVER THEIR PROPERTY AND MONEY

This form lets a person give power to someone to let them do things with the person's money, property, debt, and other things. Many people call this form the "Financial Power of Attorney" form.

FORM GIVES POWER TO LET SOMEONE CONTROL PROPERTY AND MONEY

The form lets a person (who is called in the form the "Principal") give power to someone (who is called in the form the "Agent" or "Attorney-in-Fact") to control the person's money, property, and other things. Doing this form can let the Agent for a person help use accounts, pay bills, buy or sell things, sign contracts, take out debt, hire workers, and get information from banks and others. Often named as Agent is a trusted person like a spouse, other relative, or a close friend. Doing this form might avoid need for a nursing home, guardian, conservator, or other serious thing. This form is called a "general" power of attorney since the power given is broad covering many areas, and the form is called "durable" since power of the form continues even if a person is later incapacitated. Note, a person until they are incapacitated can just overrule their Agent or fire the Agent by canceling the form if they notice a problem.

CAN GIVE INSTRUCTIONS OR LIMIT POWERS BUT FEW PEOPLE DO THIS

People can modify the form to add instructions or limit powers, but this is rare and full power is often given since the person named is trusted and banks and others may not obey the form if things aren't clear.

DUE TO RISKS MANY SKIP THIS FORM OR CONSULT A LAWYER

Many people skip this form or first see a lawyer. Using this form is risky and can lead to major harm since the Agent can be waste money, commit fraud or theft, or by carelessness allow some other harms. An Agent has a duty to be loyal and act reasonably and can be sued for any harm, but they may later be out of money to pay for misconduct. Usually banks and others can't be blamed for obeying an Agent's orders. The law is complex and basic acts of an Agent may be fine like paying bills, but some acts may be improper like making gifts, risky investments, or unusual acts. It is best a person not the Agent does anything unusual.

PERSON SIGNS FORM WITH A NOTARY

This form must be signed by a person when in front of a person who is a notary, and then the notary notarizes and also signs. The completed form can be kept by a person till needed but often it is quickly given to the Agent getting power to use if needed. To cancel the form a person usually tells the Agent it is canceled and takes back any copies and also maybe tells all places that saw the form that it is canceled.

DURABLE GENERAL POWER OF ATTORNEY

NOTICE: POWERS GRANTED BY THIS ARE VERY BROAD AND SWEEPING. IF YOU HAVE QUESTIONS ABOUT THIS DOCUMENT SEEK LEGAL ADVICE. THIS DOCUMENT DOES NOT LET ANYONE TO MAKE HEALTH CARE DECISIONS FOR YOU. YOU MAY REVOKE THIS DOCUMENT AT ANY TIME.

I, _____ of _____ County, Missouri, as the Principal making this Power of Attorney do hereby name and appoint _____ of _____ County, Missouri, as my Attorney-in-Fact. I give my Attorney-in-Fact full power, authority, and discretion to do and perform all and every act or other thing as I might or could do if personally present, including they are given general power to act. This power of attorney is effective immediately when Principal signs this document.

THIS IS A DURABLE POWER OF ATTORNEY AND THE AUTHORITY OF MY ATTORNEY IN FACT SHALL NOT TERMINATE IF I BECOME DISABLED OR INCAPACITATED OR IN THE EVENT OF LATER UNCERTAINTY AS TO WHETHER I AM DEAD OR ALIVE.

IN WITNESS WHEREOF, I sign this document on _____ 20___.

Signature: _____

STATE OF MISSOURI)
COUNTY OF _____) ss.

Before me, the undersigned, a Notary Public in and for said State, on this day personally appeared _____, personally known to me or proved to me on the basis of satisfactory evidence to be the individual whose name is subscribed to the foregoing instrument as Principal.

Given under my hand and seal of office, on the ____ day of _____, 20___.

Notary Signature: _____

CHAPTER 14
FORM 8: POWER OF ATTORNEY OVER MINOR CHILD

FORM LETS PARENT GIVE POWER TO SOMEONE OVER MINOR CHILD

This form lets a parent give power over a minor child under 18 to someone to let them help if needed.

FORM LETS SOMEONE GET POWER TO MAKE DECISIONS ABOUT A CHILD

In this form a parent can give someone power over a minor child. This kind of legal document giving power to a person is called a "Power of Attorney" and person getting power is called the "Attorney-in-Fact". This form can let someone like a friend, relative, or teacher if needed control a child's health care, school, home, discipline, and more. This form is often used if parent or child is away from the other for work, school, sports, drug treatment, prison or jail, immigration, military, month long visit with family or friends, or if a child is sick in hospital and needs someone with power close by. The form is not usually done for minor situations like a babysitter, daycare, week with relative, or any time a parent can come fast. Using this form can avoid need for much more serious actions like temporary custody or a guardianship. A parent can usually fire the Attorney-in-Fact or overrule a decision so <u>really power is shared</u>.

PERSON SIGNS FORM WITH A NOTARY

This form must be signed by a person when in front of a person who is a notary, and then the notary notarizes and also signs. The form can be modified to let a 2nd parent also sign to make it likelier doctors, schools, and others trust the form, or modified to let a legal guardian who is not a parent use this form. The form when completed can be kept by a parent until needed but often it is quickly given to person getting power to use if needed. Some parents quickly show the form to schools and doctors so they are more prepared to follow it later. To cancel the form a parent usually tells the person who got power and takes back copies and maybe tells other people that saw the form. Usually a form is done for 1 child but it can be modified to cover many children. At end of the form is an "Acceptance" spot for the person getting power to sign which can be done later.

POWER OF ATTORNEY OVER MINOR CHILD

I, who have a full name of _____, an address of _____, and telephone number of _____, am a parent in Missouri of the minor child with a full name of _____ born on _____, and I make this Power of Attorney document.

I hereby appoint the person who has a full name of _____, an address of _____, and telephone number of _____, as my Attorney-in-Fact with the power and authority described in this Power of Attorney document.

I delegate to the Attorney-in-Fact named above all of my power and authority regarding the care, custody, and property of each minor child named above including, but not limited to, the right to enroll the child in school, inspect and obtain copies of education and other records concerning the child, the right to give or withhold any consent or waiver with respect to school activities, medical and dental treatment, and any other activity, function, or treatment that may concern the child. This delegation shall not include the power or authority to consent to marriage or adoption of the child, the performance or inducement of an abortion on or for the child, or the termination of parental rights to the child.

I give my Attorney-in-Fact full power, authority, and discretion to do and perform all and every act or other thing as I might or could do if personally present at the time except no power is given consent to marriage or adoption, performance or inducement of an abortion, or termination of parental rights.

This Power of Attorney shall be in full force and effect for 1 year after signing.

The delegation in this Power of Attorney may be revoked at any time.

THIS IS A DURABLE POWER OF ATTORNEY AND THE AUTHORITY OF MY ATTORNEY IN FACT SHALL NOT TERMINATE IF I BECOME DISABLED OR INCAPACITATED OR IN THE EVENT OF LATER UNCERTAINTY AS TO WHETHER I AM DEAD OR ALIVE.

This document is governed by the laws of the State of Missouri.

IN WITNESS WHEREOF, I sign this document on _____ 20___.

Signature: _____

STATE OF MISSOURI)
COUNTY OF _____) ss.

On the date of _____ personally appeared before me _____, personally known to me or proved to me on the basis of satisfactory evidence to be the individual whose signed this document above.

Notary Signature: _____

ACCEPTANCE BY ATTORNEY-IN-FACT

The undersigned person acknowledges and executes this Power of Attorney and affirm they accept the appointment as Attorney-in-Fact and understand their duties.

Signature: _____ Date: _____

CHAPTER 15
FORM 9: POWER OF ATTORNEY FOR
RIGHT OF SEPULCHER OVER BODILY REMAINS

LETS PERSON BE NAMED TO CONTROL FUNERAL AND RELATED MATTERS

This form lets a person be named to later control funeral and related matters like burial, cremation, ceremonies, and more. Control over a dead body is called in Missouri the right to "sepulcher" which in the Latin language means "burial place".

FORM CAN NAME PERSON TO CONTROL DEAD BODY AND GIVE INSTRUCTIONS

This form lets a person <u>give power to someone to later have the "Right to Sepulcher" which is control over burial place and related things like the body, cremation, ceremonies, tombstone, and buying things for all this</u>. If this form is not done by law control is by closest family (in order this is any spouse, adult child, parents, and brothers/sisters). <u>In reality people do this form rarely</u>, usually only if it seems family may be too upset while mourning, be bad with money, or do unwanted things. Payment for things will come from any pre-paid funeral accounts, insurance, and the decedent's or estate's money and property, and Executor and family legally must help arrange payment. <u>The form also has spot to write instructions</u> but many people skip this and trust the person given power to be wise or do what was discussed. Some people do instructions to urge low cost, like to instruct people to quickly ask for "Direct Burial" or "Direct Cremation" (this is done without any delay and without family watching). Note, by law all people including family legally <u>should do the funeral, burial, ceremonies including dinners, and related things the dead person wanted if decedent's estate can afford it</u>.

SIGN FORM WITH NOTARY AND 2 WITNESSES

The form must be signed by a person in front of a notary who then notarizes it. A person should be sure to keep the form in a place it can be found within days of a death. It may help to tell someone where to find the form, or just give the form to someone to hold on to. A person can cancel the form by ripping it up, throwing it away, or clearly saying so, and then maybe telling all persons who have been shown the form.

POWER OF ATTORNEY FOR
RIGHT OF SEPULCHER OVER BODILY REMAINS

I, _____ of _____ County, Missouri, as the **Principal** making this **Power of Attorney** do hereby name and appoint _____ of _____ County, Missouri, as my **Attorney-in-Fact**.

I give my Attorney-in-Fact full power, authority, and discretion involving the Right of Sepulcher involving my bodily remains after my death and also over all related things including funeral, burial, cremation, religious services, ceremonies, food and music and readings and persons to use at events, tombstone or marker, and purchasing goods and services for all these things.

Instructions (Optional): _____
_____
_____
_____
_____
_____.

The Personal Representative handling my estate after my death and all my property and money, and also my family, by law must assist and arrange payment for things that my Attorney-in-Fact requests.

This document is effective immediately and shall not lapse including due to death.

IN WITNESS WHEREOF, I sign this document on _____ 20___.

Signature: _____

STATE OF MISSOURI)
COUNTY OF _____) ss.

On the ____ day of _____, 20____, personally appeared before me _____, personally known to me or proved to me on the basis of satisfactory evidence to be the individual whose signed this document, and they acknowledged it as their free act and deed.

Notary Signature: _____

APPENDIX:
SAMPLE FILLED OUT LEGAL FORMS

TO GET FORMS TO USE PEOPLE CAN:
  (1) PHOTOCOPY BOOK PAGES,
  (2) TEAR OUT PAGES FROM A BOOK, OR
  (3) DOWNLOAD BOOK WITH FORMS FROM WWW.DAVENPORTPUBLISHING.COM,
  AND USUALLY USING PDF FORM IS BEST TO AVOID SPACING/FORMAT CHANGES.

EMAIL ANY COMMENTS TO DAVENPORTPRESS@GMAIL.COM.

On the next pages to show how it can be done are some sample filled out legal forms.

People can add words to legal forms by computer or typewriter to be neater, but many people just by hand use pen, marker, or pencil to handwrite words into forms.

It is not required but better if signatures and dates are in ink or marker (not pencil).

Many parts of the forms especially spaces for Will gifts can be left empty and unfilled.

Anyone can fill in the words in a legal form not just the person doing the form, like a friend with neat writing can fill in all the words, addresses, and dates that are needed. Only the signatures must be done by each person doing the form for themselves.

When adding words in a form any of these is a fine way to do this:
  "I appoint ___*John Doe*___ as Agent",
  "I appoint ___John Doe___ as Agent",
  "I appoint John Doe as Agent".

When doing forms it may help to know "respectively" means "in the order just stated".

People need not worry about neatness or small mistakes, and a document is usually fine if those people who knew person during their life can tell the likely meaning.

Sample Filled Out Form : Will (Standard)
with Gifts section skipped to not bother making small gifts
LAST WILL AND TESTAMENT

I, __Paul Samuel Maxwell__, of __Cole County__, Missouri do revoke all prior Wills and testamentary documents and do make, publish, and declare this as my Will. I am of sound mind and under no duress or undue influence and acting voluntarily.

1. LIVING SPOUSE AND CHILDREN. To show I am mentally fit and have sufficient memory to do a Will I do say I now have the following living spouse and living children:

_____ none _____
_____.

2. GIFTS. I give these gifts in this Will, but to get a gift in this section the recipient must survive me except as otherwise stated below.

I give _____ to _____.
I give _____ to _____.
I give _____ to _____.
I give _____ to _____.
I give _____ to _____.
I give _____ to _____.

SKIPPED

3. SEPARATE WRITINGS. I may do writings separate from this Will to gift tangible personal property as allowed by state law, and all such writings should be followed. But any such writing not found within 90 days of my death is canceled and has no effect. A gift in such a writing to a person who does not survive me is canceled and has no effect. This Will does not revoke any such writings that now exist.

4. RESIDUE. The rest, residue, and remainder of my estate, and anything else, I give:

  a) to __Susan Lee Maxwell my sister__ who survive me and with persons just named who survive me taking the share of non-survivors, then if anything remains

  b) to __Oscar Adam Maxwell and Mary Ann Tabor__ and if any of those just now named do not survive me their part goes to their lineal descendants per stirpes.

5. ADMINISTRATION. I nominate and appoint __Susan Lee Maxwell__ as Personal Representative including for me, my Will, and my estate.

6. MISCELLANEOUS. The following applies to this Will and generally.

In this Will no part left unfilled is a mistake including spaces in the residue clause.

The facts support and I want Missouri state law to apply to this Will and my estate.

I order that my just debts, funeral and related expenses, and taxes be paid as soon after my death as practical but only those items my Personal Representative chooses to pay.

Priority of Will gifts of the same type is based on the order they are written.

The words "give" and "gift" also means a devise, bequest, grant, legacy, or similar.

I am intentionally not providing by Will or other ways for some family, including I am not providing for some children of mine and also children of a deceased child of mine.

If a gift Will reasonably mentions survival then survival is an absolute condition and anti-lapse laws or similar provisions have no effect and without survival the gift lapses. Unless a Will gift specifies otherwise if a Will gift goes to multiple recipients if any do not survive me the part to them lapses and instead goes to other surviving recipients.

No earlier transfer reduces a Will gift unless I usually called it a loan or advancement.

In this Will any gender or gendered word includes all genders, and the singular includes the plural and vice versa, and "they" can mean a single person or many persons.

Unless a Will specifically says otherwise a secured debt including a mortgage or lien shall not be paid off including by a Personal Representative or in probate, and a recipient of a Will gift of property takes it subject to debts. Also, no recipient of property who may lose it or who pays to keep it may have my estate or others pay or do exoneration.

If during my life I disposed of an item in a specific gift then the gift is extinguished.

I request and authorize any informal, summary, and quick probate or similar action. Any Personal Representative may act independently with no supervision of any court, including independent administration, and with no inventory, appraisal, or other action.

I give any Personal Representative the a) fullest authority, discretion, and powers allowed by state law, b) power to lease, sell, mortgage, convey, or keep property including real property in a manner and time they deem helpful or proper, and c) authority to settle or pay claims or debts in the time and manner they choose. Any Personal Representative or other fiduciary shall have all powers and authorities conferred by statute or common law in any jurisdiction they may act, including powers and authorities conferred by state law.

Any Guardian of any type, Conservator, Custodian, or other person managing a minor's property or money may use or invade the principal and sell property without court action.

If context permits the terms Personal Representative and Executor and Administrator are interchangeable, Conservator and Guardian of the Estate and Guardian of Property and Custodian are interchangeable, and residue and residuary are interchangeable. Any such person may stand in the place of and have all powers like the others named here.

The residue includes lapsed or failed gifts, insurance paid to the estate, digital assets, inheritances owed me, and all I had power of appointment or testamentary disposition over.

Any Personal Representative may access, manage, delete, modify, transfer, and otherwise control any digital accounts and assets I had any interest in or power over.

Any Personal Representative, Executor, Administrator, Guardian of any type like for

a person or estate, Conservator, Custodian, and any other fiduciary under this Will or otherwise shall qualify and serve without bond, surety, security, surety bond, or similar.

If evidence does not show it likely a person survived me by 120 hours (5 days) then for this Will and my estate they shall be deemed in all ways as having died before me.

If part of this Will is by law invalid or unenforceable other provisions remain in effect.

Any Personal Representative may at any time transfer money or property of a minor under age 18 to a Custodian to serve under the Missouri Uniform Transfers to Minors Act or similar law anywhere, and may pick a person to be Custodian including themselves.

TESTATOR

IN WITNESS WHEREOF, I declare and publish that this instrument is my Will which I make as Testator and I now voluntarily sign on the _8th_ day of _June_, 20_22_.

Paul Samuel Maxwell
Signature of Testator

WITNESSES

We, the undersigned Witnesses, declared the foregoing instrument was published, declared, and signed by the Testator in our presence to be the Will of the Testator, and we certify that the Testator appeared in all ways to be of sound and disposing mind and memory at the time and over the age of 18 years, and we sign our names hereunto acting to witness the Will at the request and in the presence of the Testator, and in the presence of each other on the _8th_ day of _June_, 20_22_.

Susan Ann Moon   14 2nd St., Springfield, MO 63373
Signature of Witness #1   Address of Witness #1

Eve Mable Walker   35 Buffalo Road, Denver, Colorado 80101
Signature of Witness #2   Address of Witness #2

Sample Filled Out Form : Will (Guardian)
with many gifts written in Gifts section, Guardian Clause used, and Residue Clause using percentages

LAST WILL AND TESTAMENT

I, __Paul Brian Baker__ of __Joplin__, Missouri, do revoke all prior Wills and testamentary documents and do make, publish, and declare this as my Will. I am of sound mind and under no duress or undue influence and acting voluntarily.

1. LIVING SPOUSE AND CHILDREN. To show I am mentally fit and have sufficient memory to do a Will I do say I now have the following living spouse and living children:

__Ruth May Baker wife__   __Oscar Elliot Baker young son__
__Karen Lisa Lundy daughter__   __Derek Rupert Baker son__.

2. GIFTS. I give these gifts in this Will, but to get a gift in this section the recipient must survive me except as otherwise stated below.

I give __big oak table__ to __Anne J. Smith__.

I give __$5,000 and Ford Truck__ to __Loretta Marsha Baxter__.

I give __buildings, land, and fixtures at 63 Wentworth Road, St. Louis, Missouri,__ to __Kenneth Alan Ford__.

I give __all real property and fixtures I own in Cole County in Missouri__ to __Amy Marie Fox and Pamela Sue Fox__.

I give __903 Iceberg Road, Anchorage, Alaska__ to __James Eric Hanson__.

I give __Irish jewelry and my wedding ring__ to __Mary Natalie Swanson__.

I give __all jewelry not given above__ to __Kay Baxter and Mary Baxter__.

I give __$781.35__ to __Mary Natalie Swanson and Kevin Kilby__.

I give __Wells Fargo acct ending in #8923__ to __Lawrence Deer a hunting buddy__.

I give __all spare tires and auto parts__ to __Victor Perez my mechanic__.

3. SEPARATE WRITINGS. I may do writings separate from this Will to gift tangible personal property as allowed by state law, and all such writings should be followed. But any such writing not found within 90 days of my death is canceled and has no effect. A gift in such a writing to a person who does not survive me is canceled and has no effect. This Will does not revoke any such writings that now exist.

4. RESIDUE. The rest, residue, and remainder of my estate, and anything else, I give:
   a) to _____Ruth May Baker_____ who survive me and with persons just named who survive me taking the share of non-survivors, then if anything remains
   b) to _50% to Oscar Elliot Baker, 35% to Karen Lisa Lundy, 5% to Mary Sue Baker, and 10% to Luis Sanchez my friend_____ and if any of those just now named do not survive me their part goes to their lineal descendants per stirpes.

5. ADMINISTRATION. I nominate and appoint __Ruth May Baker_____ as Personal Representative including for me, my Will, and my estate.

6. GUARDIAN. I name, nominate, and appoint _Amanda Sue Brubaker my sister_ to be Guardian of any minor child of mine and to have care, authority, custody, and other control of them. I also name this same person to be Conservator for any minor child and to have care, control, and power over their property, money, and estate.

7. MISCELLANEOUS. The following applies to this Will and generally.
   In this Will no part left unfilled is a mistake including spaces in the residue clause.
   The facts support and I want Missouri state law to apply to this Will and my estate.
   I order that my just debts, funeral and related expenses, and taxes be paid as soon after my death as practical but only those items my Personal Representative chooses to pay.
   Priority of Will gifts of the same type is based on the order they are written.
   The words "give" and "gift" also means a devise, bequest, grant, legacy, or similar.
   I am intentionally not providing by Will or other ways for some family, including I am not providing for some children of mine and also children of a deceased child of mine.
   If a gift Will reasonably mentions survival then survival is an absolute condition and anti-lapse laws or similar provisions have no effect and without survival the gift lapses. Unless a Will gift specifies otherwise if a Will gift goes to multiple recipients if any do not survive me the part to them lapses and instead goes to other surviving recipients.
   No earlier transfer reduces a Will gift unless I usually called it a loan or advancement.
   In this Will any gender or gendered word includes all genders, and the singular includes the plural and vice versa, and "they" can mean a single person or many persons.
   Unless a Will specifically says otherwise a secured debt including a mortgage or lien shall not be paid off including by a Personal Representative or in probate, and a recipient of a Will gift of property takes it subject to debts. Also, no recipient of property who may lose it or who pays to keep it may have my estate or others pay or do exoneration.
   If during my life I disposed of an item in a specific gift then the gift is extinguished.
   I request and authorize any informal, summary, and quick probate or similar action. Any Personal Representative may act independently with no supervision of any court, including independent administration, and with no inventory, appraisal, or other action.
   I give any Personal Representative the a) fullest authority, discretion, and powers allowed by state law, b) power to lease, sell, mortgage, convey, or keep property including

real property in a manner and time they deem helpful or proper, and c) authority to settle or pay claims or debts in the time and manner they choose. Any Personal Representative or other fiduciary shall have all powers and authorities conferred by statute or common law in any jurisdiction they may act, including powers and authorities conferred by state law.

Any Guardian of any type, Conservator, Custodian, or other person managing a minor's property or money may use or invade the principal and sell property without court action.

The residue includes lapsed or failed gifts, insurance paid to the estate, digital assets, inheritances owed me, and all I had power of appointment or testamentary disposition over.

Any Personal Representative may access, manage, delete, modify, transfer, and otherwise control any digital accounts and assets I had any interest in or power over.

Any Personal Representative, Executor, Administrator, Guardian of any type like for a person or estate, Conservator, Custodian, and any other fiduciary under this Will or otherwise shall qualify and serve without bond, surety, security, surety bond, or similar.

If evidence does not show it likely a person survived me by 120 hours (5 days) then for this Will and my estate they shall be deemed in all ways as having died before me.

If part of this Will is by law invalid or unenforceable other provisions remain in effect.

Any Personal Representative may at any time transfer money or property of a minor under age 18 to a Custodian to serve under the Missouri Uniform Transfers to Minors Act or similar law anywhere, and may pick a person to be Custodian including themselves.

TESTATOR

IN WITNESS WHEREOF, I declare and publish that this instrument is my Will which I make as Testator and I now voluntarily sign on the _30th_ day of _December_, 20_21_.

Paul Brian Baker
Signature of Testator

WITNESSES

We, the undersigned Witnesses, declared the foregoing instrument was published, declared, and signed by the Testator in our presence to be the Will of the Testator, and we certify that the Testator appeared in all ways to be of sound and disposing mind and memory at the time and over the age of 18 years, and we sign our names hereunto acting to witness the Will at the request and in the presence of the Testator, and in the presence of each other on the _30th_ day of _December_, 20_21_.

Olivia Anna Paulson   _82 Forest Road, Columbia, MO 63314_
Signature of Witness #1   Address of Witness #1

Matthew John Paulson   _82 Forest Road, Columbia, MO 63314_
Signature of Witness #2   Address of Witness #2

Sample Filled Out Form : Will (Guardian) with Gifts section left unused and, then, the Residue done only using 2nd space so as to gift to all branches of descendants equally

LAST WILL AND TESTAMENT

I, __Thomas Barry Tedford__ of __St. Charles County__ , Missouri do revoke all prior Wills and testamentary documents and do make, publish, and declare this as my Will. I am of sound mind and under no duress or undue influence and acting voluntarily.

1. LIVING SPOUSE AND CHILDREN. To show I am mentally fit and have sufficient memory to do a Will I do say I now have the following living spouse and living children:
_____Mary Paula Tedford my daughter_____Gina Lola Smith my daughter_____
_____.

2. GIFTS. I give these gifts in this Will, but to get a gift in this section the recipient must survive me except as otherwise stated below.

I give _____ to _____.
I give _____ to _____.
I give _____ to _____.
I give _____ to _____.
I give _____ to _____.
I give _____ to _____.

3. SEPARATE WRITINGS. I may do writings separate from this Will to gift tangible personal property as allowed by state law, and all such writings should be followed. But any such writing not found within 90 days of my death is canceled and has no effect. A gift in such a writing to a person who does not survive me is canceled and has no effect. This Will does not revoke any such writings that now exist.

4. RESIDUE. The rest, residue, and remainder of my estate, and anything else, I give:
  a) to _____ who survive me and with persons just named who survive me taking the share of non-survivors, then if anything remains
  b) to __Brian Thomas Tedford my son, Mary Paula Tedford my daughter, and__
__Gina Lola Smith my daughter__ and if any of those just now named do not survive me their part goes to their lineal descendants per stirpes.

5. ADMINISTRATION. I nominate and appoint   Mary Paula Tedford
as Personal Representative including for me, my Will, and my estate.

6. MISCELLANEOUS. The following applies to this Will and generally.

In this Will no part left unfilled is a mistake including spaces in the residue clause.

The facts support and I want Missouri state law to apply to this Will and my estate.

I order that my just debts, funeral and related expenses, and taxes be paid as soon after my death as practical but only those items my Personal Representative chooses to pay.

Priority of Will gifts of the same type is based on the order they are written.

The words "give" and "gift" also means a devise, bequest, grant, legacy, or similar.

I am intentionally not providing by Will or other ways for some family, including I am not providing for some children of mine and also children of a deceased child of mine.

If a gift Will reasonably mentions survival then survival is an absolute condition and anti-lapse laws or similar provisions have no effect and without survival the gift lapses. Unless a Will gift specifies otherwise if a Will gift goes to multiple recipients if any do not survive me the part to them lapses and instead goes to other surviving recipients.

No earlier transfer reduces a Will gift unless I usually called it a loan or advancement.

In this Will any gender or gendered word includes all genders, and the singular includes the plural and vice versa, and "they" can mean a single person or many persons.

Unless a Will specifically says otherwise a secured debt including a mortgage or lien shall not be paid off including by a Personal Representative or in probate, and a recipient of a Will gift of property takes it subject to debts. Also, no recipient of property who may lose it or who pays to keep it may have my estate or others pay or do exoneration.

If during my life I disposed of an item in a specific gift then the gift is extinguished.

I request and authorize any informal, summary, and quick probate or similar action. Any Personal Representative may act independently with no supervision of any court, including independent administration, and with no inventory, appraisal, or other action.

I give any Personal Representative the a) fullest authority, discretion, and powers allowed by state law, b) power to lease, sell, mortgage, convey, or keep property including real property in a manner and time they deem helpful or proper, and c) authority to settle or pay claims or debts in the time and manner they choose. Any Personal Representative or other fiduciary shall have all powers and authorities conferred by statute or common law in any jurisdiction they may act, including powers and authorities conferred by state law.

Any Guardian of any type, Conservator, Custodian, or other person managing a minor's property or money may use or invade the principal and sell property without court action.

The residue includes lapsed or failed gifts, insurance paid to the estate, digital assets, inheritances owed me, and all I had power of appointment or testamentary disposition over.

Any Personal Representative may access, manage, delete, modify, transfer, and otherwise control any digital accounts and assets I had any interest in or power over.

Any Personal Representative, Executor, Administrator, Guardian of any type like for a person or estate, Conservator, Custodian, and any other fiduciary under this Will or

otherwise shall qualify and serve without bond, surety, security, surety bond, or similar.

If evidence does not show it likely a person survived me by 120 hours (5 days) then for this Will and my estate they shall be deemed in all ways as having died before me.

If part of this Will is by law invalid or unenforceable other provisions remain in effect.

Any Personal Representative may at any time transfer money or property of a minor under age 18 to a Custodian to serve under the Missouri Uniform Transfers to Minors Act or similar law anywhere, and may pick a person to be Custodian including themselves.

TESTATOR

IN WITNESS WHEREOF, I declare and publish that this instrument is my Will which I make as Testator and I now voluntarily sign on the _15th_ day of ____March____, 20_21_.

Thomas Barry Tedford
Signature of Testator

WITNESSES

We, the undersigned Witnesses, declared the foregoing instrument was published, declared, and signed by the Testator in our presence to be the Will of the Testator, and we certify that the Testator appeared in all ways to be of sound and disposing mind and memory at the time and over the age of 18 years, and we sign our names hereunto acting to witness the Will at the request and in the presence of the Testator, and in the presence of each other on the _15th_ day of _March_, 20_21_.

Maria Bonita Buena   101 Fox Rd., Apt. #35 Clayton, MO 63314
Signature of Witness #1   Address of Witness #1

Richard Max West   28 Miller Avenue, Pineville, MO 63114
Signature of Witness #2   Address of Witness #2

Sample Filled Out Form : Will (Standard) with Will modified to have a 1 Part Residue Clause

LAST WILL AND TESTAMENT

I, __John David Smith__, of __Franklin County__, Missouri, do revoke all prior Wills and testamentary documents and do make, publish, and declare this as my Will. I am of sound mind and under no duress or undue influence and acting voluntarily.

1. LIVING SPOUSE AND CHILDREN. To show I am mentally fit and have sufficient memory to do a Will I do say I now have the following living spouse and living children:

__my son Adam Michael Smith__

2. GIFTS. I give these gifts in this Will, but to get a gift in this section the recipient must survive me except as otherwise stated below.

I give __$200__ to __each of my nieces and nephews so about $2,800 in total__.

I give __$400__ to __Garner Food Shelf in Cape Girardeau, Missouri__.

I give __$340__ to __my old church Salem Christian Church in Pueblo, Colorado__.

I give _____ to _____.

I give _____ to _____.

I give _____ to _____.

I give _____ to _____.

I give _____ to _____.

I give _____ to _____.

I give _____ to _____.

3. SEPARATE WRITINGS. I may do writings separate from this Will to gift tangible personal property as allowed by state law, and all such writings should be followed. But any such writing not found within 90 days of my death is canceled and has no effect. A gift in such a writing to a person who does not survive me is canceled and has no effect. This Will does not revoke any such writings that now exist.

4. RESIDUE. The rest, residue, and remainder of my estate, and anything else, I give to: ___Adam Michael Smith___ and ___Judy Paula Ford___ who survive me and if any of those just named do not survive me their part goes to their lineal descendants per stirpes.

5. ADMINISTRATION. I nominate and appoint ___Judy Paula Ford my sister___ as Personal Representative including for me, my Will, and my estate.

6. MISCELLANEOUS. The following applies to this Will and generally.

In this Will no part left unfilled is a mistake including spaces in the residue clause.

The facts support and I want Missouri state law to apply to this Will and my estate.

I order that my just debts, funeral and related expenses, and taxes be paid as soon after my death as practical but only those items my Personal Representative chooses to pay.

Priority of Will gifts of the same type is based on the order they are written.

The words "give" and "gift" also means a devise, bequest, grant, legacy, or similar.

I am intentionally not providing by Will or other ways for some family, including I am not providing for some children of mine and also children of a deceased child of mine.

If a gift Will reasonably mentions survival then survival is an absolute condition and anti-lapse laws or similar provisions have no effect and without survival the gift lapses. Unless a Will gift specifies otherwise if a Will gift goes to multiple recipients if any do not survive me the part to them lapses and instead goes to other surviving recipients.

No earlier transfer reduces a Will gift unless I usually called it a loan or advancement.

In this Will any gender or gendered word includes all genders, and the singular includes the plural and vice versa, and "they" can mean a single person or many persons.

Unless a Will specifically says otherwise a secured debt including a mortgage or lien shall not be paid off including by a Personal Representative or in probate, and a recipient of a Will gift of property takes it subject to debts. Also, no recipient of property who may lose it or who pays to keep it may have my estate or others pay or do exoneration.

If during my life I disposed of an item in a specific gift then the gift is extinguished.

I request and authorize any informal, summary, and quick probate or similar action. Any Personal Representative may act independently with no supervision of any court, including independent administration, and with no inventory, appraisal, or other action.

I give any Personal Representative the a) fullest authority, discretion, and powers allowed by state law, b) power to lease, sell, mortgage, convey, or keep property including real property in a manner and time they deem helpful or proper, and c) authority to settle or pay claims or debts in the time and manner they choose. Any Personal Representative or other fiduciary shall have all powers and authorities conferred by statute or common law in any jurisdiction they may act, including powers and authorities conferred by state law.

Any Guardian of any type, Conservator, Custodian, or other person managing a minor's property or money may use or invade the principal and sell property without court action.

If context permits the terms Personal Representative and Executor and Administrator are interchangeable, Conservator and Guardian of the Estate and Guardian of Property and

Custodian are interchangeable, and residue and residuary are interchangeable. Any such person may stand in the place of and have all powers like the others named here.

The residue includes lapsed or failed gifts, insurance paid to the estate, digital assets, inheritances owed me, and all I had power of appointment or testamentary disposition over.

Any Personal Representative may access, manage, delete, modify, transfer, and otherwise control any digital accounts and assets I had any interest in or power over.

Any Personal Representative, Executor, Administrator, Guardian of any type like for a person or estate, Conservator, Custodian, and any other fiduciary under this Will or otherwise shall qualify and serve without bond, surety, security, surety bond, or similar.

If evidence does not show it likely a person survived me by 120 hours (5 days) then for this Will and my estate they shall be deemed in all ways as having died before me.

If part of this Will is by law invalid or unenforceable other provisions remain in effect.

Any Personal Representative may at any time transfer money or property of a minor under age 18 to a Custodian to serve under the Missouri Uniform Transfers to Minors Act or similar law anywhere, and may pick a person to be Custodian including themselves.

TESTATOR

IN WITNESS WHEREOF, I declare and publish that this instrument is my Will which I make as Testator and I now voluntarily sign on the _21st_ day of ___June___, 20_23_.

John David Smith
Testator Signature

WITNESSES

We, the undersigned Witnesses, declared the foregoing instrument was published, declared, and signed by the Testator in our presence to be the Will of the Testator, and we certify that the Testator appeared in all ways to be of sound and disposing mind and memory at the time and over the age of 18 years, and we sign our names hereunto acting to witness the Will at the request and in the presence of the Testator, and in the presence of each other on the _21st_ day of ___June___, 20_23_.

Mark Elliot Potter   24 Spruce St, Sherwood, MO 63016
Signature of Witness #1   Address of Witness #1

Ann Paula Blom   80 Oak Road, Edison, MO 63972
Signature of Witness #2   Address of Witness #2

Sample Filled Out Form : Self-Proving Affidavit

SELF-PROVING AFFIDAVIT

THE STATE OF MISSOURI   )
) ss.
COUNTY OF _Franklin County_)

We, ___John David Smith___, ___Mark Elliot Potter___, and ___Ann Paula Blom___ the Testator and the Witnesses, respectively, whose names are signed to the attached or foregoing instrument, being first duly sworn, do hereby declare to the undersigned authority that the Testator signed and executed the instrument as the Will of Testator and that the Testator had signed willingly, and that the Testator executed it as the Testator's free and voluntary act for the purposes therein expressed, and each of the Witnesses, in the presence and hearing of the Testator, signed the Will acting as witness and that to the best of each of the Witness' knowledge the Testator was at the time 18 years of age or older, of sound mind, and under no constraint or undue influence.

John David Smith
Testator

Mark Elliot Potter
Witness

Ann Paula Blom
Witness

STATE OF MISSOURI   )
) ss.
CITY OF _Franklin County_   )

The foregoing instrument was acknowledged before me this _21st_ day of ___June___, 20_23_, by ___John David Smith___, the Testator and ___Mark Elliot Potter___ and ___Anna Paula Blom___, the Witnesses.

Thomas M. Shaw
Notary Public

THOMAS M. SHAW
Notary Public-Notary Seal
STATE OF MISSOURI
Commissioned for Callaway County
My Commission Expires: September 17, 2036
ID. #46746340304

Sample Filled Out Form : Tangible Personal Property Memorandum

TANGIBLE PERSONAL PROPERTY MEMORANDUM

In this writing are gifts of tangible personal property to occur at my death, but this writing if not found by someone within 90 days of my death is canceled.

I may do many pages of these writings which should all be seen as one document. If there are conflicts among such writings the provisions of the more recent writing will revoke the inconsistent provisions of a prior writing.

If a person getting a gift below does not survive me such gift is void and canceled.

DESCRIPTION OF PROPERTY	NAME OF PERSONS TO GET PROPERTY
1998 Ford Truck	to Samantha Bell
1.3 carat diamond ring + Irish rings	to Ann Sue Reed
14 ft power boat + kayak + paddles	to L. Wheeler
Amish style bench	to Reba Stewart
glass table, telescope, umbrellas	to Rebecca Stewart
Irish wood cups, oak platter, red vase	to Mary and Cindy Lott
painting of sailboat in storm	to Mary Lott
chainsaw with number 382937	to Mary Lott
chainsaw with number 89930	to Matt Smith
antique lanterns + repair kits	to Sue Wu maid at Hart Hotel
lamp kept on porch	to Mary Kay Poppler
sewing machines	to Mary Kay Poppler
rocking chair bought in Oregon	to Don Winkler boat mechanic
all fishing poles and fishing nets	to Joe "Fish" Hoss, fishing pal
hats at cabin	to Ken Baker
all clothing except hats at cabin	to Melissa and Wendy Smith
	to
	to

DATE: 5-15-2024   SIGNED: John David Smith

www.ingramcontent.com/pod-product-compliance
Lightning Source LLC
Chambersburg PA
CBHW060417220526
45465CB00008B/2924